The Biblical Marriage
For God or Government?

By:
Joshua Paul

DEDICATION

I dedicate this book to the Lord Jesus Christ. Secondly, I dedicate this book to the individuals seeking biblical insight on the topic of marriage with regards to the legalities surrounding the nature of this relationship. I dedicate this book to the people out there who believe holy matrimony is worth fighting for. I dedicate this book to those who believe that no matter how perverse, twisted and corrupt society becomes there is still a hope, faith and belief that what Jesus Christ died for is relevant more than ever in this very hour. I dedicate this book to those married couples who have been through thick and thin and overcame situation after situation by God's mercy, together. I dedicate the book to singles wondering if there is someone else out there who will love them, stick with them, seek to understand them, not give up even when their darkest, scariest fear is exposed, that no matter what life brings, someone else is there to help give the burden back to Jesus Christ, the King of Glory. I dedicate this book to those who think marriage between one man and one woman is a thing of the past and irrelevant. I dedicate this book to those who experienced a broken home, no dad or no mom or some kind of abuse growing up. I dedicate this book to those living the homosexual lifestyle wondering what the Christian perspective might look like surrounding this thing called marriage and beyond that, this thing called life. No matter who you are or what you've experienced in this great, awful, challenging, messy, chaotic life so far, it is my hope that this book might paint a picture of God's love for people, marriage, righteousness, purity and forgiveness through the Man – Christ Jesus. Hope is not lost or dead. Hope is alive today!

CONTENTS

Joshua Paul

#1 Amazon Best Seller Award

"Wow Wow Wow Wow!!!!

I was absolutely astonished at how well researched it was. It took me a while to read as my husband wanted to read it with me. Too many books identify a problem and do not offer solutions. The entire book was so incredible. I must admit that the Bible is the only book that I have ever highlighted and I have to say that in this book, I highlighted so many awesome points that I had to eventually quit because half of every page was bright yellow!! I resorted to paragraph brackets. Seriously, it has changed my husband's view and reassured him on our right and Spirit led decision.

We both learned so much and are so grateful for the book.

What a timely message!!! Definitely recommending it to all of my friends!" - L. Sipe

"Joshua has written a challenging book for all married Christians and those considering marriage. Those who desire to honor G-d in their marriage would be wise to get this book." – D. Spitz

ACKNOWLEDGMENTS

Thank you to my friends and family who encouraged me in this project. I am thankful for my parent's support, prayers and encouragement. Thank you Mom and Dad for your perspective in the face of tough decisions. Thank you to all the people who read, gave feedback and edited this book. Thank you to all the people who have shared their experiences, wisdom and insight on the intricacies of marriage.

Here is a small list of people I am thankful for in this journey, in no particular order:

Tony
Dallas
Tom
Trish
Louie
Doug
Teresa
Jim H.
James T.
James W.
Steve and Marcy
Casey
Lauren
Dave and Joy
Michael P.
Vivian
Corrie

I have learned from each of you and am grateful.

1

THE QUESTION

"Tell us, therefore, what do You think? Is it lawful to pay taxes to Caesar, or not?" But Jesus perceived their wickedness, and said, "Why do you test Me, you hypocrites? "Show Me the tax money." So they brought Him a denarius. And He said to them, "Whose image and inscription is this?" They said to Him, "Caesar's." And He said to them, "Render therefore to Caesar the things that are Caesar's, and to God the things that are God's." – Matthew 22:17-21 (NKJV)

"Caesar's," they replied. Then he said to them, "Give to Caesar what is Caesar's, and to God what is God's." - Matthew 22:21 (NIV)

"They said to Him, Caesar's. Then He said to them, Then give to Caesar the things of Caesar, and to God the things of God." - Matthew 22:21 (The Interlinear Bible - Greek/English)

The driving force behind this book stems from one question, "What are the things we give to Caesar and what are the things we give to God?" Have you ever wondered, "What is Jesus talking about in this verse?" The Pharisees came to Jesus hoping to trap Him, as usual. Jesus opens up the conversation wider, beyond money.

For several years, I had minimal understanding as to what Jesus was talking about in His statement. "Render therefore to Caesar the things that are Caesar's, and to God the things that are God's." Notice, there are "things" that are God's and "things" that are not. Notice it is not a "thing" but "things." Notice the plurality of this statement, which means more than one item, to be given to God or Caesar as the case might be.

Clearly, I understood that we are to pay taxes that are due by law to Caesar (i.e. the government). My heart's meditation was and is, "What belongs to God? What do I give to Him? What do I want to give to Him? What would He consider His?"

Maybe you figured out the answer sooner. I seriously questioned this "Caesar" topic for a long time and continue to press in for deeper revelation of this verse. The Holy Spirit revealed more of what Jesus meant. God wants us! He wants our devotion! He wants our prayer! He wants our worship! He wants our marriages! He wants our families! He wants our ministries! He wants relationship!

The Journey Begins...

In 2008, I pondered some of the things that "belong to God." For example, I began questioning the reason why Christian ministries apply for a "501(c)(3)" tax-exempt status corporate structure. According to the United States Constitution the people of God have the right to gather freely as a church. Why have a covenant agreement with the state or government at all? It did not and does not make sense to me. I thought, "If I had a ministry, then I would give that to God, not the state." In researching the legal ramifications of the 501(c)(3) status, several points of contention surfaced. A couple of the issues are limitations on freedom of speech and the state being head of the corporation through means of a contractual agreement. Jesus is left out entirely. Such ideas are completely unnecessary for any Bible believing church in the USA.

As I discovered the tremendous pitfalls of the 501(c)(3) pertaining to the Church's contractual agreement, I began to wonder, "Why the marriage license?" The line of thinking that took me from ministry to marriage was pondering the idea, "What else is the government involved in unnecessarily?" If we have rights and freedoms as United States citizens, under the governing authority of the Constitution, "Why do I need a 'license' in the context of holy matrimony? If marriage started in Eden, why the 'marriage license' now? Did George Washington, Abraham Lincoln or Thomas Jefferson have a marriage license? If they did not have a marriage license, why do I need one? Do I really 'need' one?"

Meditating further on, "Give to Caesar what is Caesar's and God that which is God's," it is clear the state marriage license and certificate gives that which is God's to Caesar. We, as a people, are covenanting or contracting with the state, not God. What gives the state corporation, government, the "right" to license marriage? The government did not and does not create marriage. What gives it the right to license something it did not create? Only the Living God can bring man and woman together. Could some of these issues be contributing to the breakdown of the family unit? These are the questions I began to ask, as the LORD focused my attention on the subject of marriage and family.

The purpose of this book is to explore the Word of God, the laws of the land and the past, present and future of marriage. The goal will be to gain knowledge, understanding, and wisdom. How are Christians to enter marriage, rightly, in the sight of God, while obeying the laws of the land? Establishing long-lasting marriages and families, is vital for the well-being of our children and our grandchildren.

"So then, they are no longer two but one flesh. Therefore what God has joined together, let not man separate." (Matthew 19:6 NKJV)

Joshua Paul

2

THE JOURNEY CONTINUES

While investigating the "marriage license," it became clear, that I wanted my marriage to be set apart to God alone. I did not have all the answers back then, however, I did have enough insight to know this was a bad deal, all the way around. There had to be an alternative to the marriage license. I did not want the state to be a part of my marriage, based on Jesus' statements regarding Caesar. (For the record, I am in favor of a marital agreement between husband, wife and the Living God. This will be discussed in later chapters.)

In July 2009, I found myself dating a wonderful young lady. Her twin brother and I already had an established friendship. I had expressed my views on the state marriage license to her twin brother, which he had subsequently passed on to his sister months before our relationship began. Even at that time, she thought not wanting a marriage license was a little odd.

Early on in our relationship I had asked, "Are you okay with not having a marriage license?" I do not recall the exact quote, but she did affirm that she was okay entering marriage without signing a marriage license. If she had not been comfortable with this idea, I would have ended the relationship and would not have gone any further than a friendship, due to my convictions on this issue.

The legalities of marriage are simply not talked about from the pulpit or around the dinner table. The American Church, for the most part, is completely ignorant surrounding the legalities of the state marriage license. I was in uncharted waters, without much in the way of a life-raft, regarding this topic. My desire was simple, to give God all of my marriage, without any strings to anything or anyone else, besides my future wife of course.

I proposed to this young lady at the beginning of 2011 in front of her parents and younger brother. She accepted. In the excitement of the engagement, we began planning the wedding, taking engagement photos and looking for a venue. However, the marriage license had not yet been openly discussed with her parents.

In May of that same year, the marriage license topic came up after church one Sunday, while at her parent's home. My future mother-in-law indicated that I could not marry her daughter without signing a marriage license. I said, "Well, at this point, I am not prepared to sign a marriage license." It became evident there was not going to be a wedding until this issue got resolved. At the time, I did not understand all of the legal ramifications of the license. I did know, God created the relationship of marriage, not the state.

During our relationship, I openly communicated my views on the marriage license with other family members, such as her uncle and younger brother. The best course of action (looking back) would have been to speak directly with her parents about my desires and beliefs. My hesitation was due to:

1. My lack of full and comprehensive understanding regarding the legalities of the marriage license.
2. Not knowing of any alternative solution to a marriage license or if there even was one?
3. My assumption that her parents knew my position and did not have an issue with it.

Several Conversations with Her Father

Several conversations ensued with my fiancé's father about the marriage license. During one particular lunch we were dialoguing about the situation. Her father stated, "My marriage is blessed. The marriage license has not had an affect on my marriage. Why didn't God tell me not to sign the license? Why did He tell you about this and not me?" I replied, "I don't know?" He followed up with, "While you're out of town, take time to ask God these questions. We'll get lunch after you get back and you can tell me what God told you." I had plans to leave town for five days. I told her father that I would pray about his questions and give him an answer upon my return. These were good, if not great questions. Admittedly, there was a bit of concern that I would not have a valid answer for him after the trip.

Thankfully, God did speak to me. I had asked the Lord, "Why didn't You tell him about the marriage license?" God's reply was humbling, "You have not, because you ask not. He never asked if he should or should not sign the marriage license. You did." Then the Holy Spirit reminded me of the book of Joshua and the story of the Gibeonites. The Gibeonites were smart. They figured if they could pretend that they were from a faraway land that the Israelites might not kill their people. Take a closer look at this story.

Joshua and the Gibeonites

3 But when the inhabitants of Gibeon heard what Joshua had done to Jericho and Ai, 4 they worked craftily, and went and pretended to be ambassadors. And they took old sacks on their donkeys, old wineskins torn and mended, 5 old and patched sandals on their feet, and old garments on themselves; and all the bread of their provision was dry and moldy. ...

7 Then the men of Israel said to the Hivites, "Perhaps you dwell among us; so how can we make a covenant with you?" 8 But they said to Joshua, "We are your servants." And Joshua said to them, "Who are you, and where do you come from?"

9 So they said to him: "From a very far country your servants have come, because of the name of the LORD your God; for we have heard of His fame, and all that He did in Egypt, 10 "and all that He did to the two kings of the Amorites who were beyond the Jordan--to Sihon king of Heshbon, and Og king of Bashan, who was at Ashtaroth.

11 "Therefore our elders and all the inhabitants of our country spoke to us, saying, 'Take provisions with you for the journey, and go to meet them, and say to them, "We are your servants; now therefore, make a covenant with us." ' 12 "This bread of ours we took hot for our provision from our houses on the day we departed to come to you. But now look, it is dry and moldy.

13 "And these wineskins which we filled were new, and see, they are torn; and these our garments and our sandals have become old because of the very long journey." 14 Then the men of Israel took some of their provisions; but they did not ask counsel of the LORD. 15 So Joshua made peace with them, and made a covenant with them to let them live; and the rulers of the congregation swore to them. ...

18 But the children of Israel did not attack them, because the rulers of the congregation had sworn to them by the LORD God of Israel. And all the congregation complained against the rulers.

19 Then all the rulers said to all the congregation, "We have sworn to them by the LORD God of Israel; now therefore, we may not touch them. ... 23 "Now therefore, you are cursed, and none of you shall be freed from being slaves--woodcutters and water carriers for the house of my God." (Joshua 9:3-5, 7-15, 18-19, 23 NKJV)

The Lord revealed something from this story, in relation to

what He had spoken previously. "You have not, because you ask not." So too, Joshua and the Israelites "*did not ask counsel of the LORD.*" Making peace with these people was not God's perfect and highest will. Joshua made an agreement that was not according to God's will, but according to his will. What can be learned from this example?

- Joshua and the Israelites moved according to their will. They failed to ask for the LORD's thoughts and opinion in the matter.

- Israel moved forward presumptuously, in covenanting with the Gibeonites.

- Israel looked at the outward appearances.

- Israel failed to accomplish God's perfect will. God's ideal and perfect will was to wipe these wicked people off the face of the earth. God gave the Gibeonites over 400 years to repent and change their ways. They did not repent.

- Israel settled for God's second best because making covenant with the Gibeonites went against God's command to wipe out all the inhabitants of the land.

24 Do not bow down before their gods or worship them or follow their practices. You must demolish them and break their sacred stones to pieces. ... 32 Do not make a covenant with them or with their gods. 33 Do not let them live in your land or they will cause you to sin against me, because the worship of their gods will certainly be a snare to you." - (Exodus 23:24, 32-33 NIV)

The LORD spoke through Moses warning not to make covenant with any people group because it would be a snare to Israel.

Were the Israelites still blessed? Absolutely. They simply did not follow God's highest and best plan for what He had in store for them in the Promised Land.

As I write this, I hear the Holy Spirit saying, "I do not want any giants in the land of My marriages. I want all the giants removed because they do not belong there in the first place. Joshua Paul, I promise you there is more to My goodness in the things of marriage and family. I promise you. Follow Me. I have more for the people of God in the things of marriage than they are currently experiencing and settling for. Do not settle."

My fiancé's father and I reconvened on the marriage license topic after my trip. I tell you with absolute assurance, I did not enjoy sharing with him the words that the Holy Spirit had spoken to me. It was humbling. It is never an easy thing to exhort a father-figure. Who am I to point out another's shortcomings? I have "planks in my own eye" to consider.

It was my hope to communicate as graciously and humbly as possible, the words that were in my heart. It went something like this: "The reason God never told you about the marriage license was because you never asked about it in the first place. You have not, because you ask not. You simply signed the piece of paper without thinking twice." I went on to say, "God showed me the example of Joshua and the Gibeonites. God's command was to wipe out all the inhabitants of the land, which included the Gibeonites, but because they failed to inquire of the LORD, they settled for less than God's perfect will. Were they still blessed? Absolutely. Was this God's perfect will? Absolutely not." I concluded by saying, "All I want to do is pursue God's perfect will, pertaining to the things of marriage."

The Beginning of the End

My fiancé and I remained engaged a few more months. Shortly following her twin brother's wedding she communicated that she wanted to be married in the next month or two. I asked, "Have your parents changed their mind regarding the marriage license?" By her response, it was clear they had not. My fiancé gave me the engagement ring back a day or two later, following this discussion.

It was now August and we were no longer together in an official relationship, but our lives were still very connected. Working for her parent's family business, we saw each other daily. Not to mention the fact that we attended the same church congregation and had the same friends. There was definitely some initial pain, but we continued talking with each other and chose to remain friends.

In December 2011, things came to a head. It became apparent that our situation was unhealthy. We were spending too much time together due to all of our mutual connections.

One day we met at the office and discussed all that was transpiring. She told me, "I need to heal and move on. Your presence is a hindrance to me." She stated, "I need to ask you to find work somewhere else in the next month or two." At one point the comment was made, "If you could just disappear from my life, that would be great." I also had a phone conversation with her Mom that same day. She asked, "Joshua have you changed your mind regarding the marriage license?"

I replied, "No. Have you?" She stated, "No, and we are not going to." That sealed the fact - I was never going to marry this girl.

I stopped working for the company immediately and communicated with her father that I needed to discontinue working at the business, for the sake of his daughter's heart.

Following Jesus' Word and His Holy Spirit is always the best choice, no matter how intense the decision. To this day, I truly believe the outcome was God's perfect will for us. I needed to follow my convictions. If I compromised on this issue, it would have been disastrous for the two of us. Never compromise your convictions as long as they are founded in Jesus Christ. Stand firm, even if the world is against you. "Greater is He that is in you, than he who is in the world."

It was a tough time, filled with introspection, crying out to God and asking questions like, "Why me?" "Why do I have to be the guy who won't sign the marriage license?"

I could identify with aspects of these Scriptures:

34 "Do not think that I came to bring peace on earth. I did not come to bring peace but a sword. 35 "For I have come to 'set a man against his father, a daughter against her mother, and a daughter-in-law against her mother-in-law'; 36 "and 'a man's enemies will be those of his own household.' 37 "He who loves father or mother more than Me is not worthy of Me. And he who loves son or daughter more than Me is not worthy of Me. 38 "And he who does not take his cross and follow after Me is not worthy of Me." (Matthew 10:34-38 NKJV)"

11 Blessed are you when they revile and persecute you, and say all kinds of evil against you falsely for My sake....

44 "But I say to you, love your enemies, bless those who curse you, do good to those who hate you, and pray for those who spitefully use you and persecute you, (Matthew 5:11, 44 NKJV)

20 "Remember the word that I said to you, 'A servant is not greater than his master.' If they persecuted Me, they will also persecute you. If they kept My word, they will keep yours also. (John 15:20 NKJV)

Through all of this, the Lord showed Himself strong. As I began to pray, search the scriptures and do more research, on this topic everything became clear. God was communicating this perspective is in alignment with His heart. Sometimes we need to take a stand in the face of opposition.

In March 2012, I found myself at a Vineyard Church in Southern California. Nobody knew me, I was simply enjoying the worship service on a Monday night. After worship, the pastor pointed at me and said, "... The Lord says about you, you're a man of integrity. You've had to make some really difficult choices lately, but those choices are choices that will pay off in the future. Just choose Jesus every time. I believe the Lord has a wonderful anointing on your life. I can see a sword on you. It is like the Spirit of Truth. I think you have a way with the truth and the Word of God that's been really precious to you. I can feel that word on you. The word of truth ... "

These words were comforting. It was clear, I did the right thing not signing the marriage license and choosing Jesus. The pastor's words were simply one confirmation.

Hindsight 20-20

I never imagined being in an engagement that would end under such unusual circumstances. Leaving my ex-fiancé's world, forced me to draw closer to God. Throughout the process of seeking, knocking and asking why all of this took place, questions came to mind, "Was it all just a waste of time? What was the purpose of all this? Did I hear You clearly?" The Holy Spirit spoke to me a few key thoughts, in the process of closing my heart to the idea of marrying this girl. He showed me that the purpose of all this was to give my ex-fiancé, her family and myself the opportunity "to mine the depths of love." I had to learn to forgive and continue loving them. They had to do the same. Truthfully, I believe they did a better job demonstrating love than I did. Each of us grew, in our own ways, regarding what it means to love like Jesus.

We parted ways from a place of purity. Praise God!

Joshua Paul

3

WHERE DID MARRIAGE ORIGINATE?

LORD, what is this thing called "marriage?" Where did it originate? It seemed important to go back to the beginning of this idea, seeking understanding for the original intent of matrimony. The Bible is the book most fitting for learning where marriage originated as this book describes the beginning of all creation.

Take a look at Genesis Chapter 2.

18 And the LORD God said, "It is not good that man should be alone; I will make him a helper comparable to him."

21 And the LORD God caused a deep sleep to fall on Adam, and he slept; and He took one of his ribs, and closed up the flesh in its place. 22 Then the rib which the LORD God had taken from man He made into a woman, and He brought her to the man. 23 And Adam said: "This is now bone of my bones And flesh of my flesh; She shall be called Woman, Because she was taken out of Man." 24 Therefore a man shall leave his

*father and mother and be joined to his wife, and they shall become one flesh.
25 And they were both naked, the man and his wife, and were not
ashamed.(Genesis 2:18; 21-25 NKJV)*

It was God's realization and understanding that man should not
be alone. God formed Eve out of Adam's rib. He then brought
Eve to Adam and Adam recognized Eve as a "woman"
distinctly for him. While it is clear, there was no "wedding
ceremony," there was in fact, a wedding and marriage
established. Adam and Eve were equally yoked, two perfect
specimens created for one another. There is no chance Adam
would have mistaken Eve for another species. God formed the
two of them and brought them together. He and all of Heaven
witnessed this momentous occasion!

Notice Genesis 2:25, that gives the recognition of marriage,
"and they were both naked, <u>the man and his wife</u>, and were not
ashamed."

Looking at the definition of wife and marriage, will help gain
greater insight into what is being stated.

Merriam-Webster defines the following:

Wife[1]:1. a married woman; the woman someone is married to
2. female partner in a marriage

Marriage[2]: 1. the state of being united to a person of the
opposite sex as husband or wife in a consensual and contractual
relationship recognized by law ...

God designed and defined marriage. Marital relationship is for a
male and a female committed to life-long commitment, living
together, and in most cases, developing a family.

---

[1] Wife "By permission. From Merriam-Webster's Collegiate® Dictionary, 11th Edition ©2015 by
Merriam-Webster, Inc. (www.Merriam-Webster.com)."

[2] "By permission. From Merriam-Webster's Collegiate® Dictionary, 11th Edition ©2015 by Merriam-
Webster, Inc. (www.Merriam-Webster.com)."

4

THE PURPOSE OF MARRIAGE

The last chapter explored the first marriage. Adam and Eve were brought together by the Living God, in the Garden of Eden. What was God's main purpose in the marriage relationship?

In the book of Genesis, God gives His command to Noah and essentially all of humanity. He tells Noah twice to "be fruitful and multiply."

1 So God blessed Noah and his sons, and said to them: "Be fruitful and multiply, and fill the earth. ...

7 And as for you, be fruitful and multiply; Bring forth abundantly in the earth And multiply in it."(Genesis 9:1, 7 NKJV)

Here God declares the purpose of humanity, to be fruitful and multiply. In order to follow this command, it requires male and female marriage relationships. The Bible continuously communicates this point throughout the entire book. The function and purpose of marriage, leads to family and the populating of the earth. Families are the bedrock of society. They keep towns, cities, regions and countries together. If the family unit breaks down, so does all of humanity.

God did not say, "Be fruitful and add." In today's industrialized, postmodern society there is concern regarding overpopulation. All of the non-biblical arguments as to why people should not have big families, are part of Satan's attack on humanity. Sadly, the Church seems to have bought into such propaganda.

China is a perfect example of population control. In fact, their society's motto would accurately be communicated as, "Be fruitful and subtract." With two people, having only one child this is the reality of what has been taking place for decades. For United States citizens, it would seem odd to have no aunts, uncles, cousins or siblings, as China currently experiences. Yet, even here in the USA people are having 1.9 children on average, per household, according to Wikipedia[3]. In the 1950's the average woman had four children.

Here is one verse that accurately depicts God's perspective regarding children.

3 Behold, children are a heritage from the LORD, The fruit of the womb is a reward. (Psalm 127:3 NKJV)

Carbon Footprint Argument

From a biblical standpoint, the "carbon footprint" argument is irrelevant when it comes to the topic of having children. God never indicated a number in which the earth would have too many people occupying it. He simply stated, "multiply" without any restriction in the context of the male and female marriage relationship. The idea of "carbon footprint," conveys the idea that there are too many people on the planet because of the

---

[3] http://en.wikipedia.org/wiki/Total_fertility_rate

large consumption of fossil fuels. The argument is then made that people need to limit the amount of children they have, as is the case in China.

In the USA, people are able to have as many children as "they choose," even though there is propaganda encouraging couples to only have one or two. God's command, be fruitful and multiply, still applies just as much today as it did in the book of Genesis. With that being said, mankind does have a duty to steward the resources of the earth and not ruin the environment. Stewardship of the earth and procreation are two independent ideas. Simply stated in the context of marriage and family, couples are to multiply.

If mankind were living according to His Word in righteousness, there would not be the issues or concerns humanity is currently facing. Ultimately, sin, such as corruption, wickedness and greed, have caused shortages of food, water and resources. The truth is, Jesus gave mankind everything necessary to live an abundant life, to thrive and fill the earth without restraint or hindrance.

Here is one powerful promise:

13 "When I shut up heaven and there is no rain, or command the locusts to devour the land, or send pestilence among My people, 14 "if My people who are called by My name will humble themselves, and pray and seek My face, and turn from their wicked ways, then I will hear from heaven, and will forgive their sin and heal their land. 15 "Now My eyes will be open and My ears attentive to prayer made in this place. (2 Chronicles 7:13-15 NKJV)

The people of God are increasing across the face of the earth. The Kingdom of Heaven is ever-increasing. There will be a profound shift regarding the increase of the land, healing and life. This will come about powerfully as people change their ways, beliefs and attitudes, to become more like Jesus and His righteousness. People will work together, grow food, and flourish. All that needs to happen is for people to simply follow the Word of God more closely.

There is no lack in Heaven. Sin is what mankind needs to point their finger at, if there is a shortage of resource in any capacity. The "carbon footprint" message is really communicating that there are too many people living without understanding of God's word. People however, can change their wicked ways. Somewhere along the way, mankind became industrialized, losing sight of God's first and original command to humanity. Please do not buy into this lie of limiting children because of a supposed shortage of earth's resources. Rather, what if mankind could have as many children as God permits and took care of the earth's resources much better. God will make a way and provide for His people. He is really big and powerful!

Godly Offspring

The Creator desires godly offspring. The book of Malachi expresses this fact. He wants marriages to be filled with fruitfulness. Children are to be instructed and raised in the Word of God. Procreation is one of the most, if not the most, significant purposes or elements of marriage because without it mankind would cease to exist.

10 Have we not all one Father? Has not one God created us? Why do we deal treacherously with one another By profaning the covenant of the fathers?

11 Judah has dealt treacherously, And an abomination has been committed in Israel and in Jerusalem, For Judah has profaned The LORD's holy institution which He loves: He has married the daughter of a foreign god.

12 May the LORD cut off from the tents of Jacob The man who does this, being awake and aware, Yet who brings an offering to the LORD of hosts!

13 And this is the second thing you do: You cover the altar of the LORD with tears, With weeping and crying; So He does not regard the offering anymore, Nor receive it with goodwill from your hands.

14 Yet you say, "For what reason?" Because the LORD has been witness Between you and the wife of your youth, With whom you have dealt treacherously; Yet she is your companion And your wife by covenant.

15 But did He not make them one, Having a remnant of the Spirit? And why one? He seeks godly offspring. Therefore take heed to your spirit, And let none deal treacherously with the wife of his youth.

16 "For the LORD God of Israel says That He hates divorce, For it covers one's garment with violence," Says the LORD of hosts. "Therefore take heed to your spirit, That you do not deal treacherously." (Malachi 2:10-16 NKJV)

The book of Malachi paints a picture of the importance of covenant, godly offspring and how much God hates divorce. The Lord is saying so much in these verses. Adultery, keeping one's covenant, not dealing treacherously with each other or the wife of your youth, are all highlighted in Scripture. Notice how God identifies divorce as an act of violence. Could divorce be related similarly to the act of Cain spilling his brother Abel's blood? Divorce is violent. What a concept to think of, divorce and violence being associated together. At the very least, keeping our commitments, contracts and covenants are highly important to God.

Birth Control, Biblical or Unbiblical?

Birth control is also worth mentioning, as one challenge within our modern society, as to the reason the Church, in particular, has stopped having big families. The Bible clearly indicates that the Lord opens and closes the womb. Why does our society think using pills to stop women's bodies from functioning as the Most High intended, is supposedly a good thing? Nothing has changed in the way God has constructed humanity. Marriage and procreation is part of the plan. His commands on the subject are everlasting.

There is a documentary on the subject called, "Birth Control - How did we get here?" You can find a copy of this film at, www.thebirthcontrolmovie.com. The production offers a great overview as to the history of how birth control came to be so popular today and in particular within the Church. It is quite an eye-opening lesson to watch and it is sobering to learn how much ungodly propaganda surrounds the topic of children in this day and age.

Condoms and Diaphragms

When discussing condoms and diaphragms things get somewhat more "grey" as to what is okay or not. The story of Onan is the only example that is loosely related to this topic. He was suppose to give his brother's wife a child, as was the custom regarding a widow with no offspring.

9 But Onan knew that the heir would not be his; and it came to pass, when he went in to his brother's wife, that he emitted on the ground, lest he should give an heir to his brother. 10 And the thing which he did displeased the LORD; therefore He killed him also. (Genesis 38:9-10 NKJV)

What displeased the LORD? It seems as though redirecting the emission onto the ground, with the intention of not impregnating his brother's wife, is what displeased the LORD. In God's eyes, Onan's actions and heart were incorrect. He spilled his seed on the ground because the child would have been his brother's, not his.

This story and example begs the question. Does using condoms and diaphragms look the same in God's eyes, as spilling seed onto the ground? What was the issue? Not impregnating his brother's wife? His hard heart? Perhaps a combination of actions caused the Lord to kill Onan?

Natural Family Planning

"Natural Family Planning" (NFP) has to do with recording the wife's cycle. Couples abstain from intercourse during the ovulation period. From a biblical perspective, NFP seems to make the most sense regarding birth control. Abstaining from intercourse during ovulation will most likely prevent one from getting pregnant. Yet, still gives room for conception.

5 Do not deprive one another except with consent for a time, that you may give yourselves to fasting and prayer; and come together again so that Satan does not tempt you because of your lack of self-control. (1 Corinthians 7:5 NKJV)

This scripture loosely suggests abstaining from sexual relations for birth control purposes. The couple could refrain from relations during ovulation. It's not directly contextualized using this as birth control, but to simply draw closer to the Most High God. One could make an argument, for or against birth control in this scripture reference.

Women Saved in Childbearing

Take a look at some Scripture in the New Covenant:

11 Let a woman learn in silence with all submission. 12 And I do not permit a woman to teach or to have authority over a man, but to be in silence. 13 For Adam was formed first, then Eve. 14 And Adam was not deceived, but the woman being deceived, fell into transgression. 15 Nevertheless she will be saved in childbearing if they continue in faith, love, and holiness, with self-control. (1 Timothy 2:11-15 NKJV)

It is interesting that Paul says women are saved in "childbearing." What a profound statement to make.

Childbearing saves women? Obviously it does not mean women receive eternal salvation through childbearing. Throughout Genesis and the entire Bible, women desire children. The more children, the more God was revealing His blessing upon her life, because He alone opens and closes the womb. The scripture above is no doubt a controversial one in the Church today. Some commentaries conclude, rather than teaching or holding authority over men, women should find true fulfillment in raising godly children, continuing in faith, helping their husbands and stewarding the home.

The TV show on TLC, "19 and Counting..." with the Duggar's is a reality TV Series about a Christian family who raises 19 children. Mr. and Mrs. Duggar trusted the Lord with conception, by not using birth control. It takes tremendous faith in God's ability to provide financially and His goodness upon people who trust Him with fertility. Their story is definitely an inspiration. 19 children! Wow! This family is clearly an extreme example of what it means to be fruitful and multiply. God's blessing abounds upon them.

Fact of the Matter...

It is easy for one to say, "Have as many babies as the Lord allows." This is no easy topic because there are so many factors that go into developing a family. It takes faith to follow the Living God of Abraham, Isaac and Jacob in marriage and in having children. There is a deep level of respect that is required for a husband and wife to go down this road in developing a family of any size. It is a lifelong commitment. May God's people continue to follow His Word, as much as possible, with amazing faith. May the LORD Jesus Christ speak to each individual's heart His truth, in this delicate subject of what "being fruitful and multiplying" should or shouldn't look like. Thank you for joining the process of asking the tough questions as to God's purposes in marriage.

Prayer

Father in Heaven, let Your purposes in family be fulfilled in the earth. Let Your ordained marriages and couples come together at the time You have determined. Let marriages be pure and undefiled. Let Your marriages last to the fullness of days, with godly offspring. I ask for couples to arise in the earth with maturity in Your Word, character and integrity so as to glorify Your purposes of family in the earth. Thank You for the beauty of husband and wife marital relationships. Thank You for Your goodness and endorsement upon holy matrimony. I ask all of this in Jesus' name. Amen.

5

FAMILIES & PREPARATION FOR MARRIAGE

Marriage is more than two people coming together. Marriage is about two families uniting. The old saying is true, "You don't just marry the husband or wife, as the case may be, but you marry the family too." It cannot be stressed enough, if possible, get to know the in-laws before marriage.

People will offer all kinds of advice, both good and... otherwise. "If you love one another, who cares what the parents say? Get married on your own!" This might sound like good advice or it might not. I know this is very much what the "world" would advise. To this I say, "If I do love her, I will honor her parent's wishes, not tear her family apart and if necessary remove myself from the situation. Love sacrifices its own interests for the benefit of the other." Moreover, there is a much to be said about having "agreement" and the "blessing" of the parents from both sides of the family.

It is hard to imagine marrying someone, without the parent's blessing and support. In many instances, such actions only prove to be an awful way to start a marriage and family. Agree or not, in my particular situation, I chose to honor my fiancé's parent's wishes by discontinuing to pursue their daughter.

Questions to ask about a potential spouse's family:

- Will his or her family influence the marriage relationship positively or negatively? If negatively, what boundaries need to be developed to protect the relationship? Can the negative dynamic be overcome, without harming the marriage to the extent of divorce?

- Will his or her family be dependent, requiring support initially or in the future? What is the overall scope of the need? In what way would you be responsible to assist them? Why is it necessary? What duration of time would potentially be required?

- Will the marriage be able to operate independently when it comes to decision making? Will any family members continue to "parent?" There is a difference between seeking advice from a parent verses being told how to do things, as if you were still a child.

- Are there any kind of controlling or manipulating attitudes in the family dynamic? If so, what is the plan to maturely address those issues?

- Has anyone advised that it may be necessary to move far away in order to establish the marriage, due to unhealthy family influences? There is a reason that the Word of God exhorts couples to "leave and cleave to each other." Generally the presence of parents can be and quite often is a very good thing. It is advisable to get their feedback on big decisions. There may be unhealthy areas requiring attention on the front end of the relationship. Marriage counselors sometimes advise couples to "move out of the state or country" to create healthy space, from unhealthy over-bearing parents.

- Have you counted the cost to "love" not only your spouse, but also the spouse's family?

These are simply a handful of questions to consider before marrying that special someone. A great book that helps handle family dynamics is, "Boundaries" by Henry Cloud and John Townsend. This book teaches how to say "yes" and how to say "no," which is part of setting healthy boundaries.

Preparation for Marriage

It is important for men and women to take inventory of their own lives and individual roles in preparation for marriage.

A Man's Preparation for Marriage

- Be a man of God. Lead the relationship. Set the pace and set the boundaries.

- Spend time in the Word of God, prayer and worshiping Jesus.

- Demonstrate a high level of trust, character and integrity.

  6 Likewise, exhort the young men to be sober-minded, 7 in all things showing yourself to be a pattern of good works; in doctrine showing integrity, reverence, incorruptibility, 8 sound speech that cannot be condemned, that one who is an opponent may be ashamed, having nothing evil to say of you. (Titus 2:6-8 NKJV)

- Serve well. Put other's needs and desires before your own.

- Clearly communicate intentions with her parents and

potential wife. Ask God for wisdom with the words and timing.

- Study the subject of marriage and family in the Bible.

- Walk in total purity before getting married. No pornography, no physical sexual engagement or encounters with the woman you are courting. Consider not kissing until the wedding day. Holding hands and short hugs in public is best. Spending time one-on-one, especially at night, is ill advised. Protecting this arena of relationship on the front end, will pay priceless "trust dividends" on the other side of marriage.

- Be a standard bearer of purity for the next generation. What testimony do you want to share with your children? They will follow your example. Think about a future conversation with your children about how you walked out your relationship. This ought to put a healthy desire for a high standard in your heart.

- Involve parents in the courting process. Ask them to help with accountability. Doing this, helps communicate that you are mature, a man of character and shows a level of commitment even in the early stages of courting. Keep in mind, that until the marriage is official, this girl is "your sister in Christ" and may end up being someone else's bride. Your main goal is helping her draw closer to Jesus. If it becomes clear that you are not going to get married, she ought to be a better individual, more free and healed in Christ. Imagine yourself as a protector of this young lady. As much as possible, protect her heart and who God has made her to be.

- Involve your pastor or elder in the courting process.

- Invite feedback and counsel from older, trusted men and women of God. The marriage relationship is much bigger than the two of you. A community of believers will help you walk this out in holiness. (If you are not prepared to approach a relationship in this context, consider stopping right where you are, because you may not be ready for the challenges or have the maturity required to lead a Christ-centered marriage. The objective is to go the distance, which will require perseverance. When a couple isolates, in most cases, this can be a sign of an unhealthy relationship.)

- Understand sometimes "Christians" can and do offer poor advice. People you know, love and look up to, may give bad counsel. They will be influenced by their worldview, experience and perspective on the Bible. There will be "testing" on whose advice to take and whose not to take. A great indication is to look at the person's character. Is their walk with God something to be admired? Are there areas of sin they continually operate in? How are their relationships? Be discerning as to whose counsel you receive. Do not let someone's age influence as to whether or not the advice can be trusted. There are individuals much older, who may sincerely, give poor advice and counsel. Encountering poor advice does not necessarily mean telling the individual their advice is bad. Simply thank them and put the advice on the back burner.

Be prepared, you will be greatly tested in your leadership of the relationship. In fact, the woman in your life may say or suggest things that are sinful. You will be tempted to sin, just like Adam, but you do not have to. Women are different creatures than men, so it might seem okay to them, to move forward with the suggestion. Do not fall for whatever way this suggestion might be "packaged." If she cries, because you say "no" to an idea because it is sin or could lead to sin, stand strong and be as compassionate as possible. She may not get it or like it in the moment. Leading as Christ would lead, showing compassion, mercy and love in the midst of the situation, is the right way to proceed. If she is a woman of God and you are right, she will respect you in the future even more than she does at the moment. That is what is referred to as, "Winning a girl's heart." The Lord will show Himself strong. He will reveal to her that you are trustworthy, a credible leader and capable of protecting her as well as the relationship. When God does back you up, try to avoid gloating, boasting or acting prideful. Stay humble and thank God for redeeming you in the situation.

- God is developing your character. If you make a mistake, repent. Confess your sin and depending on the depth of it, involve others. Please know there are varying degrees of making mistakes. Set your eyes on the beauty, excellence and perfection of Jesus. The Holy Spirit gives us the grace to be perfect as He is perfect, not the grace to dive head-first into sin. Ask God for wisdom and self-control.

- Ultimately, you are accountable before God and His Word. Let the fear of the Lord reign supreme over all of your decisions. Be the head of your household. Be the impeccable man of God that you are called to be. Follow the voice of the Good Shepherd. Ask Him for His counsel. His leadership is best.

- Walk like Jesus. Be holy as He is holy. Realize Ephesians 5 is what is required:

25 Husbands, love your wives, just as Christ also loved the church and gave Himself for her, 26 that He might sanctify and cleanse her with the washing of water by the word, 27 that He might present her to Himself a glorious church, not having spot or wrinkle or any such thing, but that she should be holy and without blemish. 28 So husbands ought to love their own wives as their own bodies; he who loves his wife loves himself. 29 For no one ever hated his own flesh, but nourishes and cherishes it, just as the Lord does the church. (Ephesians 5:25-29 NKJV)

A Woman's Preparation for Marriage

- Be a godly woman. Become a woman of the Word, a woman of prayer and a worshipper of Jesus.

- Study. Discover what the Word of God says about marriage.

- Find out about the integrity and character of the man you are in relationship with. It is easy to put on a "happy face" for 6-18 months in the beginning stages of the relationship. Ask tough questions, experience one another in different life scenarios, see how he deals with adversity and lastly, be patient. The "hurry spirit," is not the "Holy Spirit." I read recently in Sacred Marriage, "Find someone who suffers well." There are times in marriage when a husband and wife will be enduring a challenging season. Find someone who is not going to quit, but will actually thrive in such circumstances.

- Realize marriage is more than "feelings." Feelings and romance are important to any relationship and marriage is also a contract between two people who are committed to fulfilling different roles for a common goal. Think about your role, your husband's role and the vision for your marriage. If you do not have a vision currently, this might be a good time to develop one. Talk with the man in your life about developing a vision together. A great read on this subject is, "Longing for Eden, Embracing God's Vision in Your Marriage" by

Mike and Anne Rizzo.

- When exploring a long-term relationship, get advice from mature godly counselors. Women need advice from elders to protect from naivety and lack of discernment. This will help to determine if he is the real deal. Some men are not honest about who they truly are. Countless times men have communicated relationship with Jesus, only for the woman to realize, when it is too late, he does not have one. Advice from godly men and women will help the woman discern clearly the integrity and character of the man.

- Read the book of Esther. There are some gems regarding what it looks like to be a queen. Follow Queen Esther's example, not Queen Vashti's. Esther was willing to humble herself before God, seek advice from her elders and potentially lose her life for the sake of the nation. Vashti was rebellious, hard-hearted and selfish. She would have influenced an entire nation to rebel against the men in the land, putting all the relationships out of balance from how God intended in the Garden of Eden.

- Learn to let the man lead. Sadly, too many relationships have the woman "leading." That is not the order God created or intended within the family dynamic. People long for a society where men and women understand, value and appreciate their God-given roles. When both individuals fulfill these roles, harmony and health take place. Society is upside down and inside out in regards to what a godly marriage resembles.

- Last but not least, ladies, please do yourself and your man a favor and do not flaunt all the gifts God's blessed you with. Modesty is the best policy when it comes to the way you dress. This message is not popular in or out of the Church. Hollywood has fooled us into thinking that "skin is in." No. It's a trap.

Men are exceedingly visual creatures, beyond what you can comprehend. Save it for the other side of, "I do." Revealing "the goods," so to speak, does a couple things. If you are not in a relationship it sends the wrong message to the wrong guys. Chances are women dressing in revealing clothes will attract men who are walking in the flesh, lusting after their bodies. You might also ask yourself where this need to dress provocatively stems from (if you're one who tends to wear revealing clothing)? Take it to Jesus and let the Holy Spirit reveal the truth within your heart. Secondly, for those ladies in a relationship, it may make it more challenging for the two of you to keep things pure. Looks are important to an extent, however, 1 Peter communicates what is most pleasing to the Lord. Please, please, please realize that you are more than body parts. You're a daughter to the King of kings. You're royalty. Keep this reality, truth and perspective in mind. You are so valued for *all* God made you to be.

3 Do not let your adornment be merely outward--arranging the hair, wearing gold, or putting on fine apparel-- 4 rather let it be the hidden person of the heart, with the incorruptible beauty of a gentle and quiet spirit, which is very precious in the sight of God. – (1 Peter 3:3-4 NKJV)

1 But as for you, speak the things which are proper for sound doctrine: 2 that the older men be sober, reverent, temperate, sound in faith, in love, in patience; 3 the older women likewise, that they be reverent in behavior, not slanderers, not given to much wine, teachers of good things-- 4 that they admonish the young women to love their husbands, to love their children, 5 to be discreet, chaste, homemakers, good, obedient to their own husbands, that the word of God may not be blasphemed. (Titus 2:1-5 NKJV)

Marriage is a Commitment to be Taken Seriously

In reading this, it might seem like I am taking this whole marriage thing too seriously. It is true, I am taking it seriously, simply because our society really does not have a clue how sacred, holy matrimony is to the Living God. To be honest, I did not have a clue until I intentionally started looking closely at the Scriptures. Marriage is not a casual relationship. Things get tough and we cannot move on any time we want. The culture is full of bad examples and bad advice on the subject of marriage. Sadly, this cultural mind-set has pervaded the Church. The more serious and sober-minded we can be about our commitment going into marriage, the more whole-hearted and dedicated we will be through out the relationship.

On a lighter note, it is possible to have fun in the journey of discovering who God has for you. Enjoy the process. Christians more than anyone else on the planet, have the opportunity to enjoy the purity of relationship without compromise.

Prayer for Unmarried Couples

Father in Heaven, thank You for purity, righteous and whole relationships that You are developing in this generation. Thank You for the hunger and desire to be holy. Thank You for the beauty of holiness. Pour out Your wisdom on those desiring to marry in the days ahead. Let communication and understanding come forth between men and women. Let love and respect be a tremendous element in the marriage relationship. I ask for Holy Spirit unity like there is in Heaven and Kingdom marriages are established in the earth to the glory of Jesus Christ. I ask for couples to have discernment as to what it means to be equally yoked. Let equally yoked marriages be established in the dunamis power of the Holy Spirit. Let the motive driving the desire for couples to marry be of You Lord and not the lust of the flesh. I ask that the men of God arise in the earth to lead the family unit. Restore the family as You created it to be in the earth YHWH. Let Your love come down upon these marriages and future marriages. In Jesus Christ's name I ask. Amen.

6

HEBREW COURTSHIP & MARRIAGE FORMALITIES

How were weddings established from a Hebrew or Jewish perspective? What formalities took place within the families and culture? The concept of marriage has been a continual dialogue from Genesis to Revelation.

Wedding Covenant

In Hebrew culture, the covenant is also known as the "ketubah." The function of the ketubah is primarily for the protection of the bride. The groom and the father of the bride negotiate the terms of the "bride price" along with the roles and responsibilities of the bride and groom. All that he owns and all that she owns, become each other's. They share their mutual assets, as well as debt responsibilities.

The ketubah is written out, with specific dates, times and obligations included in the agreement. In most cases, the bride price is paid prior to the wedding. Some examples of payment might include silver, gold, cattle, real estate or work performed. Depending upon the quality of the bride, the price can vary. Some factors which may impact the bride price include: whether the woman is a virgin, the skills she possesses, her assets, any outstanding debt or other qualities of value she brings to the relationship.

At the end of the book, there is a sample of an orthodox ketubah. This particular example presents the bride price amount as a total of two hundred zuzim pieces of silver. Zuzim equals 1/4th of a shekel and 2.5 shekels go into 1 ounce. In today's terms, 20 ounces of silver equals the bride price mentioned in the example ketubah[4].

Now for a father or even a bride reading this, they may think, "She's/I'm worth way more than 20 ounces of silver." The truth is, the bride is priceless, to Jesus and hopefully to the husband as well.

In the case of Jesus and His Bride (the Church), Jesus gave His life, by death on a cross, to His Heavenly Father Father as the bride price and ransom. This redeemed humanity and reconciles man to God.

25 Husbands, love your wives, just as Christ also loved the church and gave Himself for her, - (Ephesians 5:25 NKJV)

Song of Solomon also paints a picture of the bride price.

7 Many waters cannot quench love, Nor can the floods drown it. If a man would give for love All the wealth of his house, It would be utterly despised. (Song 8:7 NKJV)

---

[4] Messianic Perspectives July-August 2011 A publication of CJF Ministries
https://www.scribd.com/fullscreen/66981748?access_key=key-
6qcykw38wo4pc7hhd0q&allow_share=true&escape=false&show_recommendations=false&view_mode
=scroll

Why the Bride Price is Important

The Word of God is filled with wisdom, offering insight on the topics of investment, time and appreciation. When an individual receives something for "free" they generally do not value it as much as if they had to work hard to "pay a price." Take a sixteen year old for example, what will the outcome likely be regarding giving them a car or making them work for a car? More often than not, it is the teenager who works hard to save money to buy their own vehicle, who truly understands the investment of time, energy and work. The one who worked and saved up for a car will likely take care of their investment much better than the one who was given the car.

In today's culture and world of the state marriage license, it costs the man very little to marry a woman. If the average cost of a state marriage license and certificate is one hundred dollars, that is a small financial commitment. It is easy for the man to walk away, as he is not vested in the long-term, well-being of his bride. Women desire to be valued and cherished. It is the way they have been designed. For a number of reasons men are leaving their wives. Notice the growing number of single moms today. Godly value needs to be restored to women.

With the bride price approach, which involves parents in the courting process, there is going to be a reduction in divorce and less men walking out on their wives. Divorce rates will decrease because a high value is placed upon the bride. This high value will sift the pretenders from the contenders. The boys with impure motives and weak character will not be able to sustain what is required to pay the high value. The men worthy of a godly woman will stay the course in the face of whatever obstacles may arise.

Exchange of Value in Every Marriage

While riding my bike one Saturday morning, I was pondering

the idea, "Why does the state care so much about licensing marriage?" The LORD revealed something I found to be of great significance. In every marriage arrangement around the world, there is always a "payment" or form of "value" exchanged between various parties. The question is, "Who are you paying and why?" The state corporation wants the bride price "compensation," which validates its "parental authority" and position in the relationship. Receiving money for the marriage license, conveys power and authority to the state. This transaction removes the necessity of parental approval. No longer are parents a requirement in the marriage process. Usually, the bride price goes to the father or parents of the daughter, but in recent times it has been going to the government. A term known as "parens patriae" makes the state, parent over the marriage. (This will be discussed further in another chapter.)

Honoring Your Parents

12 "Honor your father and your mother, that your days may be long upon the land which the LORD your God is giving you. (Exodus 20:12 NKJV)

1 Children, obey your parents in the Lord, for this is right. 2 "Honor your father and mother," which is the first commandment with promise: 3 "that it may be well with you and you may live long on the earth. (Ephesians 6:1-3 NKJV)

Going to the state, instead of the parents, may bring division between family members. If Christians esteem Bible scripture, as both Jesus and Paul did in the new covenant, then how can the Church go to the state for permission to marry? The marriage license has the ability to allow dishonor of parents, by circumventing their input into the marriage of their children. When parents are submitted to the Word of God, their insight and discernment for their child's well-being and future, should be considered as part of a decision as big as marriage. Is the author suggesting parents "force" or "arrange" marriage for their children? No. However, if parents have done a relatively decent job raising their child, the parent's approval and input ought to be welcomed.

When couples seek the state's approval and permission to enter into holy matrimony, God's process is circumvented. The intimacy of relationship between parents and children then breaks down. Imagine a couple going to the courthouse, to get an application. They fill it out and pay the license fee. There is no relationship or connectivity taking place. The application process is a cold, disconnected transaction. What is the alternative to this application process with the state? The children come to the parents. There are multiple discussions about the future of the children's lives together. There can be talks of roles and responsibilities of the husband and wife. There is the exchange of value from groom to father of the bride. There is a knitting together of families and relationships. Can such conversations still take place when the couple also apply for a state marriage license? Absolutely. The point being made is, why would anyone ask a stranger sitting next to them on a plane or a bus permission to get married?

Then take it a step further, inviting that stranger to become a part of their marriage covenant. That seems very silly and maybe a little exaggerated, but that is really what is taking place.

The Marriage License is the Bride Price – A Personal Story

One evening I was talking with the father of my ex-fiancé regarding the merits of the marriage license. This was a particularly revealing conversation. He commented, "Joshua, the marriage license has had no bearing on my marriage, whatsoever. In fact, I don't even know where it is, when it was dated or signed? It has played no role in my marriage. It means nothing to me."

The conversation continued between the two of us. I communicated some of the things that I had learned regarding the marriage license agreement with the state. My points were not well-received or considered. His fundamental response to my objection of the license was, "You have fear." At a certain point it seemed clear that he was not capable of responding to me with any response other than, "You have fear." Looking back, I would say he was right. I did have fear. The fear of the LORD. I was choosing to fear God, rather than man. I also believe that he and his wife found some kind of security in the marriage license and thought that it would protect their daughter from a legal standpoint, in the event of a divorce or some other matter. It would have been nice to simply have a sober conversation about it all. The license provides a false sense of security because people divorce for any reason these days. What I am recommending in terms of the marriage process for two believers, offers more security, commitment and depth of understanding.

As the conversation progressed, I eventually told him, "I will give you everything I own to marry your daughter." I did not have hundreds of thousands of dollars, but to give all that one has, surely must be worth something? How many men do you know who are willing to give all their wealth to marry their bride? Interestingly, her father communicated emphatically, "The bride price is the marriage license. We can do that other stuff too, if you want, but the bride price is the marriage license." I found this incredibly insightful because earlier in the conversation he told me that the marriage license meant nothing to him and his marriage. But for some reason, when it came to his daughter, it meant everything. What a dichotomy of thought.

Towards the end of the conversation, her father began to get upset and was shouting at me. I remained calm and unmoved by his mannerisms. As I sat in my seat observing and listening, I realized, "Satan REALLY does not want people to enter marriage without a marriage license." I considered this a full-on demonic manifestation because of his rage and complete lack of the fruit of the Spirit. I thought to myself, "There is no way I am going to sign a marriage license. Total confirmation." At that moment I asked him, "Why are you acting like this?" His immediate response was, "BECAUSE I'M TRYING TO GET THROUGH TO YOU!!!" I thought, "Yup, you are getting through alright, just not in the way you might be desiring."

In closing, I want to say, I love this man and his family. All of them have impacted my life in a powerful way. Truly, I will never be able to repay them for their love. In that particular conversation, a demonic spirit of intimidation, fear and control manifested. I forgave him and realized in that moment, it was not him speaking, but something else influencing him. Deep down, he loved me. This man was simply doing what he thought was best for his family's interests. Let's face it, how many fathers typically have such a conversation with a man interested in marrying their daughter? These were uncharted waters.

Hebrew Courtship - Betrothal

There are two stages to the betrothal process. The first part is the "kiddushin," which is very similar to what we would call the engagement period. However, in the Jewish community this step basically communicates the couple is now husband and wife. The second part is the nisu'in. The nisu'in is where the couple goes under the "chupah" and communicate their nuptuals[5]. Betrothal is basically a contract between the two families and sealed with the exchange of gifts. Betrothal is the uniting of not just two people, but two families. The couple does not live together or experience consummation, they are simply promised to one another. All parties involved perceive the couple as husband and wife. An example of this would be

[5] http://www.bible.ca/marriage/ancient-jewish-three-stage-weddings-and-marriage-customs-ceremony-in-the-bible.htm

Jacob and Rachel's seven year period. It was not until the seven years were completed that the two consummated the marriage. Upon consummation, the couple is considered officially married.

Kiddushin:

In the old covenant the Israelites made covenant with YHWH (God) through the Law of Moses. The Torah was essentially God's instruction book and covenant to a specific people He calls the apple of His eye.

Nisu'in:

Is the fullness of God and His people dwelling together. The Jews refer to this as the "messianic era" and believe this will be when relationship with God will become "tangible." This is where God dwells with mankind and mankind dwells with Him. Born again followers of Jesus who have been baptized into the Holy Spirit, experience the indwelling right now. Believers are the temples of the Living God, where communion with YHWH has been restored, through the finished work of the cross and Y'shua the Jewish Messiah (Jesus Christ). The old covenant has been done away with and now the new covenant is established. Currently mankind only has a deposit of things to come, because believers are waiting for the fullness of the wedding supper of the Lamb!

The Bible is truly the greatest love story ever told. The Creator of Heaven and Earth left everything for humanity. He left all the wealth, comfort and exaltation, to come down to man's level and become dirt. Humans are nothing more than clay pots. The King of Glory, left it all behind for humanity. He left it all behind to restore His people from the curse of sin and death. He rescued mankind from the disobedience that took place back in the Garden of Eden. The only thing humanity needed to do was not eat of the tree of good and evil. Apparently, that command was too difficult. Adam and Eve could not obey. God's children barely scratch the surface regarding the depth of beauty, character, nature and love, Jesus has for them.

The analogy I think of, regarding Jesus dying and saving humanity, goes something along these lines. What Jesus did for us would be similar to you or I choosing to become an ant, to save the ants, then remain an ant and marry all of the ants that chose to marry us. I mean think about it, becoming an ant is crazy! Why would I ever want to become an ant, to be with the ants forever? There is simply no way I would ever choose to become an ant. I wipe them up in my kitchen, crush them under my foot, without thinking twice. Maybe a better analogy would be a cockroach? For sure, there is no way I would ever dream of rescuing the cockroaches, let alone be married to one. Can you imagine? Yet this is a tiny comparison of Jesus' perspective towards us. WOW! We are so frail, weak and broken. He is all-powerful, all-knowing, all-loving, all-merciful, all-gracious, and the list goes on. He became a man, for us!

Preparation

There is a preparation period for the ceremony and celebration of the union. "Preparation" occurs within the betrothal period - kiddushin[6]. The groom "prepares" a place for the two to live. The length of time varies based on contractual obligations and other details that need to occur prior to the celebration and consummation of the marriage union.

Customarily today, there is preparation for the wedding ceremony; wedding clothes picked out, invitations sent to the guests, marriage counseling, finding a place to live and all of the many details leading up to a new life together.

Right now the Bride of Christ is waiting for the Bridegroom (Jesus) to return from preparing a place, in the Father's house. The Bride is in the process of making herself ready for the return of the groom.

---

[6]http://www.chabad.org/library/article_cdo/aid/477321/jewish/Kiddushin-Betrothal.htm

Celebration and Consummation

Once everything is prepared and ready, the bridegroom is released by his father to go and gather his bride to himself. Together they go to the celebration of the wedding feast. Once the ceremony is complete, the wedding feast continues while the couple goes into a special room, set apart for them, to consummate the marriage. It was of the utmost necessity to ensure that the woman be a virgin, as was laid out originally in the ketubah. The two become one flesh. They assume a new identity together. The couple has now become husband and wife.

In review of this chapter, it is clear marriage is a matter of process, purpose and testing. When God's people follow His process, seek and trust Him, stability within households comes forth in tremendous strength and virtue. Society is built upon family. In the next chapter a closer look will be taken regarding the ceremony process. Key elements will be identified necessary to establish marriage from both a biblical and a lawful perspective.

7

CEREMONY

One of the bigger questions regarding the wedding ceremony itself is, "Does there have to be a minister or a civil official present for a couple to marry?" Take a look at what scripture and U.S. law reveal, regarding the idea of having an officiate preside over a wedding ceremony.

Adam and Eve

In Adam and Eve's story, God created and brought about the marriage. God formed Eve out of Adam and brought her to him, identifying her as his wife.

21 And the LORD God caused a deep sleep to fall on Adam, and he slept; and He took one of his ribs, and closed up the flesh in its place. 22 Then the rib which the LORD God had taken from man He made into a woman, and He brought her to the man. 23 And Adam said: "This is now bone of my bones And flesh of my flesh; She shall be called Woman, Because she was taken out of Man." 24 Therefore a man shall leave his father and mother and be joined to his wife, and they shall become one flesh. 25 And they were both naked, the man and his wife, and were not ashamed. (Genesis 2:21-25 NKJV)

Adam and Eve's matrimony did not include a formal wedding ceremony or even a marriage license. They had children together which proves consummation. In verse 24, the word "wife" by definition, implies marriage. Adam and Eve lived together their entire life in a God-ordained marriage relationship.

Isaac and Rebekah

Isaac and Rebekah have a unique story. Abraham requested that his oldest servant return to the country of his family and find a wife for Isaac. Abraham's servant provided the "bride price" or valuable possessions to give to Rebekah's family. Rebekah and her family approved of the marriage to Isaac. Like Adam and Eve, God brought the woman to the man.

41 'You will be clear from this oath when you arrive among my family; for if they will not give her to you, then you will be released from my oath.' ... 51 "Here is Rebekah before you; take her and go, and let her be your master's son's wife, as the LORD has spoken." ...53 Then the servant brought out jewelry of silver, jewelry of gold, and clothing, and gave them to Rebekah. He also gave precious things to her brother and to her mother. 54 And he and the men who were with him ate and drank and stayed all night. Then they arose in the morning, and he said, "Send me away to my master." ...57 So they said, "We will call the young woman and ask her personally." 58 Then they called Rebekah and said to her, "Will you go with this man?" And she said, "I will go." 59 So they sent away Rebekah their sister and her nurse, and Abraham's servant and his men. 60 And they blessed Rebekah and said to her: "Our sister, may you become The mother of thousands of ten thousands; And may your descendants possess The gates of those who hate them." 61 Then Rebekah and her maids arose, and they rode on the camels and followed the man. So the servant took Rebekah and departed. ...63 And Isaac went out to meditate in the field in the evening; and he lifted his eyes and looked, and there, the camels were coming. 64 Then Rebekah lifted her eyes, and when she saw Isaac she dismounted from her camel; 65 for she had said to the servant, "Who is this man walking in the field to meet us?" The servant said, "It is my master." So she took a veil and covered herself. 66 And the servant told Isaac all the things that he had done. 67 Then Isaac brought her into his mother Sarah's tent; and he took Rebekah and she became his wife, and he loved her. So Isaac was comforted after his mother's death. (Genesis 24:41, 51, 53-54, 57-61, 63-67 NKJV)

Abraham believes there is a woman from his homeland suitable for Isaac. It takes tremendous faith and trust in God's ability to bring a husband and wife together. The servant, a man of faith, prays to the God of Abraham specifically about how to identify the woman for Isaac. God responds immediately to his prayer.

12 Then he said, "O LORD God of my master Abraham, please give me success this day, and show kindness to my master Abraham. 13 "Behold, here I stand by the well of water, and the daughters of the men of the city are coming out to draw water. 14 "Now let it be that the young woman to whom I say, 'Please let down your pitcher that I may drink,' and she says, 'Drink, and I will also give your camels a drink'--let her be the one You have appointed for Your servant Isaac. And by this I will know that You have shown kindness to my master." 15 And it happened, before he had finished speaking, that behold, Rebekah, who was born to Bethuel, son of Milcah, the wife of Nahor, Abraham's brother, came out with her pitcher on her shoulder. (Genesis 24:12-15 NKJV)

Only God could orchestrate such precision in the timing and response to what transpired. Rebekah's family recognized God's hand in these events. They give her away with their blessing. Rebekah was clearly a woman of faith, to say "yes" to marrying a man she had never met, who lived in a faraway land. Proposals do not often happen in such fashion. Rebekah believed God as a woman of faith, which was perfect for Isaac, the son of the "father of faith" - Abraham. The characters each demonstrated faith. God was working to accomplish His purposes.

Often in today's society people want their "freedom" to choose. Mankind was no different then. Everyone agreed with God's will. Amazing!

The "wedding ceremony" was not really a ceremony at all. Rebekah covers herself with a veil. The servant then tells Isaac about his journey. Isaac and Rebekah consummate the marriage. There was one witness, the servant. No paper work, just a verbal agreement. No audience (that was mentioned) simply an agreement between husband and wife, consummation, cohabitation and then a family. The Most High God brought these two together. "What God brings together, let no man separate."

The author of Genesis adds, "...and he loved her." This is the first time the Bible mentions love between a husband and wife. Isaac made the decision to love Rebekah, without hesitation, because she was his wife. At this point in time, she was a total stranger. Remarkable. He made a choice to love her, not based upon feelings or what modern culture uses to define love.

Jacob, Rachel and Leah

Another biblical marriage example would include Jacob, Rachel and Leah. Examine Jacob and his Uncle Laban's relationship.

15 Then Laban said to Jacob, "Because you are my relative, should you therefore serve me for nothing? Tell me, what should your wages be?"... 18 Now Jacob loved Rachel; so he said, "I will serve you seven years for Rachel your younger daughter." 19 And Laban said, "It is better that I give her to you than that I should give her to another man. Stay with me." 20 So Jacob served seven years for Rachel, and they seemed only a few days to him because of the love he had for her.21 Then Jacob said to Laban, "Give me my wife, for my days are fulfilled, that I may go in to her." 22 And Laban gathered together all the men of the place and made a feast. 23 Now it came to pass in the evening, that he took Leah his daughter and brought her to Jacob; and he went in to her. ... 25 So it came to pass in the morning, that behold, it was Leah. And he said to Laban, "What is this you have done to me? Was it not for Rachel that I served you? Why then have you deceived me?" 26 And Laban said, "It must not be done so in our country, to give the younger before the firstborn. 27 "Fulfill her week, and we will give you this one also for the service which you will serve with me still another seven years."

28 Then Jacob did so and fulfilled her week. So he gave him his daughter Rachel as wife also. ... 30 Then Jacob also went in to Rachel, and he also loved Rachel more than Leah. And he served with Laban still another seven years. (Genesis 29:15, 18-23, 25-28, 30 NKJV)

Laban asks Jacob what his wages should be. Jacob views Rachel as an asset belonging to Laban. He placed a value on Rachel as something to earn and work towards for seven years. Full-time work back then was ten hours a day, six days a week. Jacob had no other promise of wealth, until the agreement concluded. Laban covered the cost of living, but the pay-off for Jacob was Rachel. Rachel's voice in the matter is absent. Laban and Jacob define the agreement themselves. Laban says, in verse 19, "it is better I give her to you than someone else." Biblically speaking, the male family member consents and "gives" the bride to the groom. In this instance, Rachel is Laban's possession and responsibility. This "betrothal" or "engagement" period lasted for seven years. Verse 21 communicates that Jacob and Rachel did not have any sexual relations, until Jacob asked Laban for his permission to "go into Rachel." Laban throws a wedding feast and gives Jacob a bride.

In this example we learn several things:

- Bride is seen as an asset owned by the father
- Father gives permission to marry daughter
- Father and groom make verbal agreement for daughter
- Groom gives father something of value, an asset for his daughter, in this example seven years of labor for one

virgin bride

- Betrothal or engagement can be any amount of time, in this case seven years
- Consummation allowed after fulfillment of obligation
- Celebration feast with several witnesses, establishing a wedding day
- Honeymoon or wedding week, where the husband and wife spend time together alone
- No minister or civil servant mentioned in any of these three marriage examples
- No money given to the government
- Proper understanding pertaining to the laws of the land were vital

The reader can learn a lot regarding courtship, ceremony and marriage from these examples. The bible reveals subtle, yet tremendous differences in approaching the marriage relationship, legally and otherwise.

What Does U.S. Law Say About an Officiate?

Here is an excerpt from the "American Uniform Marriage and Marriage License Act," which came about in 1923 by the federal government. Items underlined are added emphasis by the author of this book. The act communicates, that any religious group of people, have the freedom to marry, without someone officiating their wedding ceremony.

"Thirty seven states provide for marriage ceremonies according to the customs rules and regulations of Quakers, and other Religious Societies. Such ceremonies are in a sense merely marriage contracts in the presence of witnesses, without being performed by or before an Officiating Person. One of the chief purposes of this Act being the procuring of a license in proper legal form, and the registration of said license, it is, of course, immaterial whether the marriage ceremony be performed by a minister or civil official or in the presence of the proper number of witnesses in conformity with the rules and regulations of the proper Religious Society.

This Clause 2 of Section I is in no sense a restriction upon, but is rather an enlargement of the provisions of Clause 1 of said Section. Clause 1 provides for the celebration of marriage before some legally authorized official, whether ecclesiastical or civil. But since Quakers, and many others, object to any form of ceremony other than that prescribed by the Religious Society to which either or both of the contracting parties may belong, it was recognized by the Conference that such persons should be permitted to enter into the marriage relation in the method prescribed or authorized by their respective religious rites and ceremonies.

Nevertheless while conceding the right of such parties to be married according to the rules and regulations of any such Religious Society without the sanction of a legalized "Officiating Person," by merely it was deemed essential that at least one of the parties should be a member of such Religious Society in order to entitle such parties to the benefit of the looser form of marriage contract authorized by said Clause 2 of Section I, which, being an exception to the general rule requiring a marriage ceremony to be performed by some "Officiating Person," should go no farther than warranted by the circumstances of the case. In other words, where a Religious Society recognizes a marriage without an Officiating Person it should do so only because such a marriage is binding on the conscience of at least one of the contracting parties as a member of the Society, and the peculiar rights and privileges which may be granted to members of Religious Societies should not be extended to those who are not members so as to allow them to take advantage of the rules of the Society to which they owe no obedience and with which they have no affiliation.

No such Society itself would celebrate a marriage unless at least one of the parties was a member of the Society. The phrase any "Religious Society Denomination or Sect" is broad enough to include not only Quakers, but every other denominational sect, or society, including the Ethical Society of New York, and other States, Christian Scientists, etc.

None of these Religious Bodies would allow interlopers to be married according to their rules and regulations when neither of the parties had any connection whatever with the organization.

Just as under Clause 1, there should be two competent witnesses, so also should there be under Clause 2, arid the parties should likewise "declare in the presence of such witnesses that they take each other as husband and wife.[7]"

Concluding Points Regarding an Officiate

The Bible and the laws of the United States of America reveal the following:

Christian couples can choose freely whether or not they want to have an officiate preside over their wedding ceremony. Couples following the Bible can opt-out of the officiate element of the ceremony because of religious freedom, communicated in this act.

Couples preferring an officiate can choose anyone from their religious society to perform the ceremony. However, if the couple also desires the officiate to sign a marriage license, that individual must adhere to proper legal procedures, communicated within each state's legislature.

Having a pastor or governmental clerk "officiate" a wedding, remains optional according to the Bible and the United States legislature. All of this is contingent upon the recognition of a

---

[7]http://www.uniformlaws.org/shared/docs/Marriage%20and%20Divorce%20Act/UMDA%201973.pdf

"Religious Society." The idea of an "officiate" has in fact become more "tradition" than something dubbed an absolute necessity. A Christian husband and wife can freely include or exclude an "officiate." Historically, either decision is legal.

8

CONCEPTION

Conception from Heaven's Perspective

While spending time with a friend of mine, I got the opportunity to hear about a vision that he once had. This vision spoke of what takes place in Heaven when a baby is conceived. He was kind enough to describe exactly what he saw:

CONCEPTION OF A CHILD

ALL HEAVEN CELEBRATES THE MOMENT

"Jesus showed me the scene and said "All heaven celebrates at the moment a child is conceived. During the celebration the angel Michael stands up, then trumpets are blown drawing attention to Michael shouting out the proclamation of the destiny of who that child is meant to be, calling them by name. Because Satan and his demons were in heaven at creation, they have the right and ability to hear these proclamations, giving them insight from conception, on how to possibly sidetrack their destiny. It is very important for fathers to pray into the destiny of their children from the moment of conception, forward. This is one of the most important responsibilities and privileges of being a father. You get to, and must help shape and form their destinies".

All things got silent and very serious when Michael stood up and the trumpets blew. It was an indication of how serious this matter is to God. I actually got to watch the celebration and proclamation of one child. People were jumping, shouting, and clapping. It went on for a while, like a group of cheerleaders, calling out the destiny that had just been proclaimed. I was amazed at how big Michael was compared to all others. He was over twenty feet tall! I also saw heaven groan over the loss of the destiny of a child aborted.[8]"

Conception of Marriage

The wedding becomes the "conception" day of a marriage and then in most cases family. Every marriage has a destiny and a day of conception. Wouldn't heaven respond in like-manner as a baby being conceived? Isn't the same idea taking place? Marriage is conceived on the wedding day of two people committing their lives to one another. God has a destiny for every marriage, because the husband and wife have a destiny. Therefore, we can conclude the two as one, have a destiny together written in heaven. Scripture confirms these ideas in Psalm 37, Psalm 139 and Jeremiah 29:11.

Two people coming together in the sight of God, is the first

---

[8] Written by T. Leverett March 22, 2010

steps in establishing godly offspring. The more people experience salvation, the more reward Jesus receives for the work He did on the Cross. Satan wants to fight God and mankind, tooth and nail, to steal Jesus' reward. Satan's entire mission is to destroy families. The oneness of marriage is a reflection of the trinity of God. There is no division, no separation, and perfect unity for the Most High. The family unit is made in the image of God and the intent of the family is perfect unity, glorifying Jesus.

Do the Actions of the State, Affect My Marriage?

Here is an analogy of how all marriages, in particular Christian marriages, are affected by the "voluntary" state marriage license. Imagine a mom who has conceived and becomes pregnant. The mom in this story represents the state. The umbilical cord represents the state marriage license. The baby represents the husband and wife marriage relationship. The state controls the marriage through the connection of the license. Whatever the state feeds on, in terms of righteous or unrighteous law, will directly pass through the umbilical cord to the baby. The state decides what to consume and the husband and wife have no voice.

Here are two examples:

1. Imagine if the mom eats healthy, organic, nutritious food, takes vitamins and minerals, predominantly drinks water, does not drink alcohol, smoke marijuana, smoke cigarettes or do drugs. The Mom lives a healthy life overall. The baby receives healthy food, nutrients, enzymes, and everything necessary to grow strong and healthy because of the umbilical cord.

2. Now, what if rather than eating healthy, the mom only eats fast food, is an alcoholic, smokes cigarettes, does drugs and participates in other harmful activities. The long-term health of the baby will likely be affected.

Primarily, everything that supports the baby's life is controlled and dictated by what the mom eats, breathes and drinks. Life or death is made in the decisions of the mom, practically speaking, because she alone chooses. Notice the tremendous responsibility the mom has for her baby's well-being. Decisions do have consequences.

Fifty or sixty years ago, the federal and state government was operating in greater alignment with godly principles and perspective. Currently, government is ever so quickly diving headfirst into unrighteousness and disagreement with the Word of God. It is disappointedly, losing sight of any moral compass and is being swayed by the popular opinions of the minority. On several occasions, the people's vote surrounding the topic of marriage has not been upheld.

The idea of government redefining the definition of marriage is flat-out awful. How much pride does it take, to think that it is possible to redefine a word that has existed since the beginning of time? This shift towards exalting wickedness is wreaking havoc on the family unit across the nation. The state marriage license covenant becomes the umbilical cord to feed the husband and wife nutrients or sludge. The demonic realm gains access to the marriage and family through the covenant agreement the marriage license represents. As the government becomes more wicked, it will become increasingly more difficult for marriages to stay together. Let's face it, marriage is challenging enough on its own. God's people do not need to be yoked to an unholy, ungodly body of law.

It seems fairly clear that Satan and the principalities and powers of darkness have set up a system to influence the marriage relationship through a legal access point. With the marriage license signed the day of the ceremony (conception of the marriage), Satan and his minions have direct access. Depending on the individuals in the relationship, there may be multiple access points – this being a significant one to any marriage. Of course Satan waits for the absolute weakest point or moment to attack. The goal is to come to that place, where like Jesus, we could say, "Satan has nothing in me."

Life is difficult as it is, for a baby to grow up, become a healthy adult and live to be 85 years old. There are natural troubles and challenges that pop up, without needing any additional help. In today's moral decline, the marriage license actually creates an unnecessary, harmful environment for a marriage to properly sustain itself on. In the second example, feeding on unhealthy poisonous toxins, is what we are seeing from the government system today. In this analogy, the state seems to increasingly feed on more and more wickedness. It my belief that this reality is damaging and harmful to the long-term goal of a healthy, life-giving marriage.

Satan on the Ground Floor

If Satan can get in on the ground floor, (i.e. through the marriage license) then the married couple has no other reality of relationship apart from life together with the license. If everyone follows the same protocol, then nobody can see a difference in relationship or question the status quo. Putting everyone in the same boat is the government's goal. The old saying is true, "Do not rock the boat." God's people, in particular, would be well-served to not yoke themselves to the unholy state and ungodly body of laws. People are beginning to see the truth, stand for freedom and the freedom of their children. The legal system right now is not a picture of freedom, it is modern day slavery. Our forefathers would be shocked to see what is taking place in this country today.

The work of Satan exists entirely in the playground of ignorance. If people continue to go along with the status quo and do not stop to think or question what is actually transpiring, then he wins.

Paraphrasing Jesus, He says, "... ask, seek, knock. You have not because you ask not." The last thing Satan wants any of us to do is ask questions.

Prayer

Jesus, I ask that You make Your people great "askers," discerning of spirits and filled with wisdom. Amen.

9

ORIGIN AND HISTORY OF MARRIAGE LICENSES

What is the Origin of State Licensing?
The origin of "state licensing" began primarily within the Roman Catholic system. In the 1500's, the Roman Catholics controlled much of life surrounding the rules and regulations of how the family unit conducted itself. Going as far back as the Council of Trent, "decrees" were passed by the Roman Catholic church, as legislature, to hedge in the Protestant movement and reform the Roman Catholic system. It was during this time period, that the Council of Trent determined marriage be conducted before the parish priest or with a license by a "non-ordained Roman Catholic priest," in the presence of witnesses.

The purpose of this legislature was to force Baptists, Protestants and others to stop marrying in their own churches. Roman Catholics worked to prevent the Protestant movement from performing their own ceremonies. Protestants had an increasing desire to separate themselves from these civil authorities and ultimately the Pope. The Pope was seen as the spiritual leader who determined the laws and regulations for all Catholics, rather than Jesus.

Eventually, groups within the Protestant reformation rejected the idea of being subject to the dictates of the Roman Catholic system and civil authorities. Couples began coming together in holy matrimony within the congregations they fellowshipped. Christians who married within their congregations were falsely accused of advocating immorality and depravity.

One such couple who married outside the Roman Catholic system was even imprisoned. In 1551, Jeronimus Segerson wrote a letter to his wife Lyksen, "Grace, peace, gladness, joy and comfort, a firm faith, good confidence, with ardent love to God, I wish my most beloved wife, Lyksen Dirks, whom I married in the presence of God and his holy church, and too thus agreeably to the Lord's command to be my wife."

She replied with the following, "My dear husband in the Lord, whom I married before God and His people, but with whom they say I have lived in adultery, because I was not married in Baal: the Lord saith, 'rejoice when men shall say all manner of evil against you; rejoice and be exceedingly glad, for great is your reward in heaven." [9]

This couple understood the ramifications of the marriage license. The license would bind them to Catholic civil authority. The outcome of this contract would make the individual subservient to whichever department or agency is tied to the license. The licensee submits to the regulations the agency had placed in the contract.

Protestants Move Away from Catholics

Why were the Protestants and Baptists so eager to get away from the Roman Catholic system or specifically their doctrine? "Aren't they all Christian?" A common misconception regarding Roman Catholic doctrine and their religious system, needs to be addressed.

---

[9]http://www.drbentownsend.com/documents/the%20marriage%20license.pdf

No doubt there are those in Catholic parishes who have relationship with Jesus and look to Him alone. However, the Roman Catholic "doctrine" (what is taught - Catechism) regarding how one must be saved and enter eternal life, communicates a false sense of salvation because it is not actual Bible Scripture. Catechism doctrine declares, "…Catechism expounds revelation..." another quote would include, "The plan of this catechism is inspired by the great tradition of catechism which build catechesis on four pillars: the baptismal profession of faith (the Creed), the sacraments of faith, the life of faith (the Commandments), and the prayer of the believer (the Lord's Prayer)." Basically, Catechism could be seen as a commentary, expounding revelation and Catholic tradition. Does every parish teach out of the Roman Catholic Catechism, God only knows? Visiting every parish is an impossibility. It is my hope that some of these parishes would have born-again believers, teaching Hebrew Scriptures and the New Testament Covenant from the Bible, not Catholic tradition in the form of Catechism.

Here is a list of truth that goes against false doctrinal teachings:

- Purgatory is not in the Bible and does not exist
- Infant baptism does not ensure salvation -Acts 8:36-37
- Praying to "virgin Mary" & the saints is idolatry –John 14:13
- Salvation is not works-based (penance) -Romans 10:9
- Pope-Pontiff – is not the bridge maker to God -Acts 4:10-12

Protestants desired to disconnect from the Roman Catholic system for various reasons, some of these reasons are mentioned above. The false teachings and overreaching control placed upon the people by the Roman Catholics, led to this divide.

Here are some links to further explore Catholic teachings:

https://carm.org/list-of-roman-catholic-false-teachings

http://www.vatican.va/archive/ENG0015/__P5.HTM
http://www.vatican.va/archive/ENG0015/_INDEX.HTM

The History of Marriage License in the USA

The founding fathers of the United States, did not want a state-church similar to England or a church-state similar to France and Spain. A notable judge from the 18th century, William Blackstone advised against civil law ideas. He stated, "The civil law was partly of pagan origin." Common law marriage originated from England in the middle ages and was adopted in this nation after the Revolutionary War. State licensing began when blacks and whites married, because at the time, this was an illegal act and illegal relationship. Licensing this type of relationship was the only alternative the government had. Eventually, the states had a meeting to abolish common law marriage all together and put marriage under statutory (civil) law. The two outcomes of the state license are a revenue stream and a system of control. The result of this decision, once again, placed married couples under civil authorities, rather than under church authority. This was a legal move to put the church under the authority of the state and civil authorities because participation was "voluntary." Any time the minister in a marriage ceremony closes with, "By the power or authority vested in me by the state of ...." the minister is now under the governor of the state's authority. There is no difference between the minister or a judicial representative of the state.

The mixture of civil law and God's law, in the arena of marriage, causes a problem because marriage is a God-given right. The state can only go so far as to simply make this issue entirely "directory" or another way of saying it, "voluntary."

The history of the marriage license was developed in the southern regions America where blacks and whites were beginning to "intermarry." North Carolina and Tennessee were two of the first states to issue a "marriage license." In the 1800's it was illegal for blacks and whites to marry. Miscegenation law is another legal term used by the government to prevent interracial marriage.

In the mid 1800's, there were approximately half a million "free negroes" in the USA. At the time, the culturally or social accepted norms at that time were that "negroes" were inferior to "whites." It was assumed that, "If someone was black, you must be a slave." Therefore, even though the Emancipation Proclamation had taken place, the "negroes" were still only free in name. The prevailing attitude of the day continued to legislate civil law, year after year, requiring "licenses" for just about anything and everything, including but not limited to: carrying papers to prove freedom, gun permits, occupational and business licensing, church congregation supervision of a licensed white minister, permits to travel freely, etc. What can be gleaned from this example? The business of licensing is used to control a group of people, through the regulations of the state. Complete freedom is not possible in such an environment. Things need to change today just as much as they did in the 1800's.[10]

Prior to this time, people were generally entering into marriage under "common law" or through unlicensed individuals performing religious ceremonies. Only a very small percentage of society was participating in miscegenation, an act that was considered illegal. Take a look at what happened in 1911, which ultimately led to the marriage license of today.

American Uniform Marriage & Marriage License Act

In 1909, several states gathered together on the topic of marriage. The purpose behind the gathering was two-fold. The first objective was to abolish the idea of common law marriage. The second objective was to make the license an absolute pre-requisite to marriage.

Read their intentions regarding their meeting:

American Uniform Marriage & Marriage License Act

---

[10] http://www.drbentownsend.com/documents/the%20marriage%20license.pdf

AN ACT

"The following Act "Relating to and Regulating Marriage and marriage licenses" was first considered by the National Conference of Commissioners on Uniform State Laws at Detroit in August, 1909.

At that meeting the Committee on Marriage and Divorce was directed so to shape the Act that <u>"Common Law Marriages" should be abolished. This was effected by making the issuance of a license to marry an absolute prerequisite (subject to one saving clause, see Section XXIV), and by requiring that the marriage be properly solemnized.</u> At the meeting of the Conference in Chattanooga in August, 1910, the Act was more or less amended, and was referred back to the Committee to incorporate the amendments and such other desired changes as they should deem advisable. At Boston in August, 1911, the Act in its present form was finally adopted, and ordered to be printed and circulated by November, 1911, for submissions to the Legislatures of the several States.

Walter George Smith- President of the Conference

Philadelphia, PA -November 1, 1911"[11]

The entire marriage license act was adopted by all 50 states in 1929. Hollywood helped propagandize the state license program in movies such as the 1934 Academy Award winning film, "It Happened One Night." The closing comments in this film end with dialogue of a married couple referring to the two stars in the movie, "I do not even think they're married?! Yes, they are. I saw the marriage license."

Miscegenation Laws Made Illegal

<u>Blacks Law defines **miscegenation**[12]</u> as, sexual relations

---

[11] American Uniform Marriage and Marriage License Act
[12] Miscegenation - by permission Blacks Law Dictionary 10th edition

between races; esp., the production of offspring by parents of different races, usu. when and where considered illegal. In 1967, the U.S. Supreme Court held that laws banning interracial marriages are unconstitutional because of Loving vs. Virginia.[13]

Uniform Marriage & Divorce Act

Eventually "The Uniform Marriage and Divorce Act" (UMDA) was established in 1970, which allowed for marriage dissolution or divorce for any reason. One individual could divorce the other without finding any fault. Prior to this act, people needed to prove fault of the other party such as desertion, adultery, alcoholism, physical abuse, etc. In Part III of the UMDA, the party leaving the marriage can also collect spousal support from the other party.

The state, while it is not suppose to be a business, very much runs as a business (that never becomes profitable). The license serves as the "product" the state is selling to citizens. Every good business wants to find ways to increase revenues. State governments have a vested interest in controlling moral activities by licensing those activities, thereby, generating income. Taxation on liquor, tobacco, gambling, prostitution are examples of activities requiring a state license.

The development of the marriage license is a means of generating substantial income for the state. Not only does the state stand to make money when the couple desires to marry, but additionally, when a couple desires to divorce. They must go to court to seek dissolution of the marriage and pay court fees, attorney fees, filing fees, etc. Each time a couple is married and divorced, the state receives more income. From a revenue standpoint, it is in the state's best interest to see marriages fail.[14]

---

[13] https://www.law.cornell.edu/supremecourt/text/388/1
[14] http://www.drbentownsend.com/documents/the%20marriage%20license.pdf

10

Parens Patriae

Parens Patriae is a term that is not too common in our culture today. However, this idea has existed for hundreds of years. This gives a history of how the state sees itself as our parent and/or our child's parent. Our individual relational status depends entirely on how we view ourselves and the agreements we sign off on.

Blacks Law Defines:

Parens Patriae[15]: Latin "parent of his or her country"

1. The state regarded as sovereign' the state in its capacity as provider of protection to those unable to care for themselves.

2. A doctrine by which a government has standing to prosecute a lawsuit on behalf of a citizen, esp. on behalf of someone who is under legal disability to prosecute the suit <parens patriae allowed the state to institute proceedings>

---

[15] By permission Blacks Law Dictionary 10th edition Dictionary

The state ordinarily has no standing to sue on behalf of its citizens, unless a separate, sovereign interest will be served by the suit.

"The *parens patriae* doctrine has its roots in English Common Law. In feudal times various obligations and powers, collectively referred to as the "royal prerogative," were reserved to the king. The king exercised these functions in his role of father of the country.

In the United States, the *parens patriae* doctrine has had its greatest application in the treatment of children, mentally ill persons, and other individuals who are legally incompetent to manage their affairs. The state is the supreme guardian of all children within its jurisdiction, and state courts have the inherent power to intervene to protect the best interests of children whose welfare is jeopardized by controversies between parents. This inherent power is generally supplemented by legislative acts that define the scope of child protection in a state.

The state, acting as *parens patriae*, can make decisions regarding mental health treatment on behalf of one who is mentally incompetent to make the decision on his or her own behalf, but the extent of the state's intrusion is limited to reasonable and necessary treatment.

The doctrine of *parens patriae* has been expanded in the United States to permit the attorney general of a state to commence litigation for the benefit of state residents for federal antitrust violations (15 U.S.C.A. § 15c). This authority is intended to further the public trust, safeguard the general and economic welfare of a state's residents, protect residents from illegal practices, and assure that the benefits of federal law are not denied to the general population.

States may also invoke *parens patriae* to protect interests such as the health, comfort, and welfare of the people, interstate water rights, and the general economy of the state. For a state to have standing to sue under the doctrine, it must be more than a nominal party without a real interest of its own and must articulate an interest apart from the interests of particular private parties.[16]"

The state, through licensing, is letting people "voluntarily" self-identify with one of the three categories:

1. Child

2. Mentally ill person

3. Legally incompetent to manage their affairs

Whichever one a person chooses, it does not matter. Therefore, they will "manage" whomever's marital relationship and affairs, as occasion arises. The state will gladly tell people what to do, when to do it, and how to do it, if allowed. Married couples who sign the marriage license are in fact giving control to the state, as if they are children, mentally ill or too incompetent to manage themselves, their marriage and their family.

Braveheart

Braveheart conveys a great example of *parens patriae*. This movie demonstrates the attitude and perspective of the state government (King Longshanks) towards the people. Through the marriage license, the people, in essence are handing-over their rights to the state. The state becomes parent to "their children" and sovereign over the marriage relationship.

In the beginning of the movie Braveheart, King Edward Longshanks communicates, "The trouble with Scotland is that it

---

[16] Reference: TheFreeDictionary © 2015 by Farlex, Inc.
http://legal-dictionary.thefreedictionary.com/Parens+Patriae

is full of Scot's. Perhaps the time has come to re-institute an old custom. Perhaps then prima nocte? First night, when any common girl inhabiting their lands is married, our nobles shall have sexual rights to her on the night of her wedding. If we cannot get them out, we will breed them out. That should fetch just the kind of lord's we want in Scotland. Taxes or no taxes, huh?"

In the following scene, a nobleman intrudes on a Scottish wedding, by announcing, "I've come to claim the right of Prima nocte. As lord of these lands I will bless this marriage by taking the Bride into my bed on the first night of her union. It is my noble right." The English nobleman claims "his right" to what in the movie is called "prima nocte or noctis." This law allows the English nobles to have sexual relations with the Scottish peasant virgins on their wedding night. The implications of this will lead the first born of all Scottish families to be of English and Scottish heritage. A bastardized nation will ensue. English and Scottish breeding cause the first born to be left without its true father, with divested loyalties and identity.

Prima nocte was a way for "government" to control marriages, families and economies. This is very much what the state is doing with the marriage license today, attaching itself to marriage. Parens patriae or prima nocte (as it is called in Braveheart) has taken place throughout history. Such ideology is one of control.

Notice, they do not simply establish a law allowing a nobleman to sleep with a peasant girl, upon becoming an adult. Why do they specifically force this issue on the night of the wedding ceremony? It is for the purpose of taking control over the family unit and marriage, while maintaining a taxable enterprise. In the past, if a man was not committed to a woman or the family, she would have less chance of survival. The ruling system cannot afford to have all the unwed women bearing children without support. The whole purpose is to maintain a system of control, so the ruling class could still tax the peasants. The nobles needed a population for support, so they themselves actually did not have to work.

The entire storyline of Braveheart is a depiction of what is transpiring in our society. Currently, the government in the USA is growing like a monster, requiring more money from the population in order to maintain control over the population. We currently experience increased taxes and more governmental jobs that do not drive an economy, but help maintain control. Elected officials receive high salaries and funding from lobbyists. The game that was played so many years ago with the nobles and peasants, still plays out today through our political system.

In Braveheart, the Scottish "nobles" (who were under the rule of the English nobles, but above the peasant class - middle class for lack of a better description) never wanted to fight for their freedom, because they could politically negotiate for more lands and titles. In essence, they were being bribed or bought off. They were happy, as long as they were cared for and not living the peasant life. The Scottish nobles had no loyalty to the common man. Loyalty only remained to their purses. William Wallace makes a speech to Scottish nobles and says to them, "You are so concerned with squabbling for the scraps from Longshanks table that you have missed your God-given right for something better. There is a difference between us. You think the people of this country exist to provide you with position. I think your position exists to provide those people with freedom and I am going to see that they have it!"

Robert the Bruce, the King-in-waiting to Scotland, follows Wallace out the door, "Wait. I respect what you said. But remember that these men have lands and cattle, much to risk."

Wallace follows up with, "And the common man that bleeds on the battlefield, does he risk less?"

A righteous government is designed to serve the needs of the people in such a way so they are free to live a life of prosperity, not oppression. When an unrighteous government is in power, the people are oppressed with taxes and unjust laws. We are seeing this take place, more and more, in this country. Currently, taxes are increasing and the civil statutes are being corrupted due to the love of money. Laws are established because special interest groups are buying politicians. Laws condoning baby killing (abortion) and sexual perversion are being accepted in various forms. Our fiat monetary system is totally corrupted. This nation is anything but free. There may not be chains and shackles hanging on our wrists and feet, but I assure you they are there through the agreements we make. The shackles just look a little different, in this digital age. The Founding Fathers and the men who fought for freedom in years gone by, would be dismayed to see the current state of affairs regarding this nation.

King Longshanks, after learning Wallace invaded the city of York, says, "I will offer a truce and buy him off." This is the state mentality. The state gives as little as it can to maintain a perception of power and control. Rather than do what is right for all the people, Longshanks is willing to give a little, to one man, Wallace, who leads the destiny of Scotland.

Somehow, the government in America has convinced the people of the supposed benefits of signing up for the state marriage license. There are no additional benefits for married couples who have signed a state marriage license versus those who have not. We are defrauded by the state into thinking there are additional benefits, when really, there are none.

As Braveheart continues, in the next scene, the Princess of

England, is sent on behalf of King Longshanks to offer the bribe to William Wallace. She says to William, "The King desires peace. He proposes you withdraw your attack. In return, he grants you title, states and this chest of gold." Wallace replies, "Lordship and titles, gold! That I should become Judas?!" The Princess replies, "Peace is made in such ways." To which Wallace quickly follows up, "Slaves are made in such ways!!!"

A Society of Virtue?

Virtue: morally good behavior or character: a good and moral quality: the good result that comes from something[17].

God intended marriage to be a holy and sacred union. Satan wants to do everything he can to throw a wrench into what God desires. The wedding day is the foundational point of the new life created between husband, wife and children to follow. This will be explored further in the next chapter.

The sad reality of the world today is that people are so easily bought off with bribes or willing to settle for much less. Ideals, integrity and justice have been so perverted by men and women who compromise for the sake of money, looking out for their own interests. Politicians have tough jobs. Sadly, it seems so many have sold out the American people to fatten their own wallets. Can we start to look out for the interests of others for the good of all? We must become a people of "virtue" again. It is disappointing to see how people have walked away from virtue and handed their freedoms over to the controlling, ruling class.

---

[17] Virtue - By permission. From Merriam-Webster's Collegiate® Dictionary, 11th Edition ©2015 by Merriam-Webster, Inc. (www.Merriam-Webster.com).

11

IS THE GOVERNMENT HOLY?

Are any of the governmental agencies, holy, according to the Word of God? Here are some definitions to help bring understanding to the idea of holy and God.

Holy[18]: exalted or worthy of complete devotion as one perfect in goodness and righteousness; divine ...

Divine[19]: of, relating to, or proceeding directly from God or a god; being a deity; directed to a deity; supremely good.

Deity[20]: the rank or essential nature of a god; a god or goddess; one exalted or revered as supremely good or powerful.

The Interlinear Bible defines holy:

Holy: apartness, sacredness, holiness

---

[18] Holy - By permission. From Merriam-Webster's Collegiate® Dictionary, 11th Edition ©2015 by Merriam-Webster, Inc. (www.Merriam-Webster.com

[19] Divine By permission. From Merriam-Webster's Collegiate® Dictionary, 11th Edition ©2015 by Merriam-Webster, Inc. (www.Merriam-Webster.com

[20] Deity - By permission. From Merriam-Webster's Collegiate® Dictionary, 11th Edition ©2015 by Merriam-Webster, Inc. (www.Merriam-Webster.com

And you shall be to Me a kingdom of priests and a holy nation.' These are the words which you shall speak to the children of Israel." – (Exodus 19:6 NKJV)

… but as He who called you is holy, you also be holy in all your conduct, because it is written, "Be holy, for I am holy." – (1 Peter 1:15-16 NKJV)

But you are a chosen generation, a royal priesthood, a holy nation, His own special people, that you may proclaim the praises of Him who called you out of darkness into His marvelous light; - (1 Peter 2:9 NKJV)

There are technically only two governments at work in the earth, the Kingdom of Heaven and the kingdom of darkness.

For we do not wrestle against flesh and blood, but against principalities, against powers, against the rulers of the darkness of this age, against spiritual hosts of wickedness in the heavenly places. (Ephesians 6:12 NKJV)

The principalities, powers and the rulers of darkness largely run the federal and state governments. The world government system is increasingly moving forward by the hand of the evil one. The good news is the Kingdom of God is advancing more deeply and powerfully than the world system ever could. Amen.

11 "Now I am no longer in the world, but these are in the world, and I come to You. Holy Father, keep through Your name those whom You have given Me, that they may be one as We are.

12 "While I was with them in the world, I kept them in Your name. Those whom You gave Me I have kept; and none of them is lost except the son of perdition, that the Scripture might be fulfilled.

13 "But now I come to You, and these things I speak in the world, that they may have My joy fulfilled in themselves.

14 "I have given them Your word; and the world has hated them because they are not of the world, just as I am not of the world.

15 "I do not pray that You should take them out of the world, but that You should keep them from the evil one.

16 "They are not of the world, just as I am not of the world.

17 "Sanctify them by Your truth. Your word is truth.

18 "As You sent Me into the world, I also have sent them into the world.

19 "And for their sakes I sanctify Myself, that they also may be sanctified by the truth. (John 17:11-19 NKJV)

Are there righteous men and women in our government? Yes. There are a some that have found the narrow path and are called to be in the world government system to influence it for the Kingdom of God. The Most High uses each of us in unique and wonderful ways.

Covenant Agreement

Whether we know it or not, couples are yoking themselves with an institution and body of law that is condoning, child sacrifice (abortion), murder, stealing, fornication, adultery and a laundry list of other sins. They are putting their marriage under a body of laws that go directly against the Word of God.

According to Black's Law Dictionary covenant is defined as:

Covenant[21]: A formal agreement or promise, usu. in a contract.

---

[21] Covenant - Permission by Black's Law Dictionary, 10th ed. 2014

Doesn't it seem as though the marriage license agreement would fall under that of a "contract" or "covenant?" Consider God's warnings and promises for His people in the old testament.

A Closer Look at Deuteronomy 7:1-16

1 "When the LORD your God brings you into the land which you go to possess, and has cast out many nations before you, the Hittites and the Girgashites and the Amorites and the Canaanites and the Perizzites and the Hivites and the Jebusites, seven nations greater and mightier than you,

Each of these nations, as well as Egypt, had their own set of laws, rules and regulations that God said were ungodly, evil and wicked. God instructed His people to live a different way, with their own statutes and judgments of righteousness.

2 "and when the LORD your God delivers them over to you, you shall conquer them and utterly destroy them. You shall make no covenant with them nor show mercy to them.

Notice how he states, "make no covenant (contract)" with them. Why do you think that is? Let us keep reading His Word for the answers.

3 "Nor shall you make marriages with them. You shall not give your daughter to their son, nor take their daughter for your son.

Interesting to point out in verse 2 - make no covenant - verse 3 - nor shall you make marriages with them. The people of God seem to be "covenanting/contracting" with other nations, another body of law outside the Word of God and "marrying with them."

4 "For they will turn your sons away from following Me, to serve other gods; so the anger of the LORD will be aroused against you and destroy you suddenly.

In the USA, children are rebelling against their parents, following the way of the world and turning their hearts away from the Living God. Some of these sins include:

- adultery
- fornication
- homosexuality
- perversion of all kinds
- pornography
- molestation
- rape
- divorce (outside the context Jesus communicates)
- children being murdered in the womb

It is virtually impossible to tangibly quantify the impact our actions have in the spirit realm. The spirit realm is more real than the things that are seen, as stated in Hebrews 11:3. No doubt, the principalities and powers are able to use our agreements to gain entry points into our lives, without our knowledge of this taking place.

5 "But thus you shall deal with them: you shall destroy their altars, and break down their sacred pillars, and cut down their wooden images, and burn their carved images with fire."

6 "For you are a holy people to the LORD your God; the LORD your God has chosen you to be a people for Himself, a special treasure above all the peoples on the face of the earth."

We are to be "holy" or "separate" to the LORD. He has chosen us for Himself, not to be shared with the other "nations." What a beautiful picture. God is jealous for us and does not want to share us with any other god, lover or nation. Let us be jealous for Him, not willing to share our affections or agreements with any entity apart from Him.

7 "The LORD did not set His love on you nor choose you because you were more in number than any other people, for you were the least of all peoples;" 8 but because the LORD loves you, and because He would keep the oath which He swore to your fathers, the LORD has brought you out with a mighty hand, and redeemed you from the house of bondage, from the hand of Pharaoh king of Egypt.

He is faithful to keep His oath and covenant (contract, pulling us out of the house of bondage. The state has become a house of bondage and a form of Egypt or Babylon.

9 "Therefore know that the LORD your God, He is God, the faithful God who keeps covenant and mercy for a thousand generations with those who love Him and keep His commandments;

God is faithful to keep His covenant. He is unchanging and faithful for a thousand generations! He is so good! Do you think the government is faithful and merciful like YHWH (Yahweh – God)? Let us choose covenant with Him.

He alone is trustworthy.

10 "and He repays those who hate Him to their face, to destroy them. He will not be slack with him who hates Him; He will repay him to his face. 11 "Therefore you shall keep the commandment, the statutes, and the judgments which I command you today, to observe them.

12 "Then it shall come to pass, because you listen to these judgments, and keep and do them, that the LORD your God will keep with you the covenant and the mercy which He swore to your fathers.

13 "And He will love you and bless you and multiply you; He will also bless the fruit of your womb and the fruit of your land, your grain and your new wine and your oil, the increase of your cattle and the offspring of your flock, in the land of which He swore to your fathers to give you.

Verse 13 has amazing promises for the family. Look at what God promises when we choose to covenant with Him. He will bring forth increase upon our lives.

14 " You shall be blessed above all peoples ; there shall not be a male or female barren among you or among your livestock.

15 "And the LORD will take away from you all sickness, and will afflict you with none of the terrible diseases of Egypt which you have known, but will lay them on all those who hate you.

16 "Also you shall destroy all the peoples whom the LORD your God delivers over to you; your eye shall have no pity on them; nor shall you serve their gods, for that will be a snare to you. (Deuteronomy 7:1-16 NKJV)

Such beautiful promises to God's people for following His Way. Following His Way, there is no need for another solution provided by the state. Let's be holy unto Him. Atheists, agnostics, unbelievers may need or desire the state's laws, statutes and judgments. God's people simply need His Word, obedience and love – we only need His way. As the book of James 1:25 describes God's law, "the perfect law of liberty." He wants to make covenant with us.

He wants to protect us. He wants to set our affections on Him alone. He wants to keep us from defilement.

Again, there is no communication piece about a state marriage license covenant in the Bible. Just because something is not discussed or mentioned, does not mean there is no context for it in society today. We drive automobiles and have driver's licenses, but there's no mention of them in the Bible. I get that argument. Some people suggest, that we should not have driver's licenses either. Such battles can be left for another conversation. The question is, what gives the state the right to license something as holy and of God, as marriage? Only God creates and establishes two people in a marriage relationship, not the state.

Remember, Jesus fulfilled the law on the cross at Calvary. I am not advocating looking to the law for salvation of sins, but as a way of living, to prevent one's self from becoming defiled by the world. Perhaps God's people have made agreements that have tied God's hands? Therefore, preventing the fullness of His blessings to flow unhindered in their lives. People make inner vows that require undoing. It makes sense that outward vows would also need to be undone. In this case, the state marriage license would be a prime example.

In conclusion, the people of God are well served to pay attention to the things they are agreeing to. Covenants are contracts, contracts are agreements and agreements are attachments. Attaching one's self to the world system seems to go against what the Bible instructs. Each individual needs to decide for themselves, what that looks like before the Lord.

It is the glory of God to conceal a matter, But the glory of kings is to search out a matter. – (Proverbs 25:2 NKJV)

12

PERMISSION FROM THE STATE

Why are those who call themselves, "The Bride of Christ" and "Followers of Jesus" going to the state for permission to marry? The reality is most of us do not understand the implications of signing the marriage license. Generally, people are simply excited to start a new chapter in life and get married. I certainly did not have any idea about the ramifications of the marriage license, until investigating the matter further. Rarely, if ever, does anyone teach what the marriage license actually represents.

There is not one biblical example of anyone ever needing a "license" or "permission" from any governing body outside of the family, to marry, until recent history. Permission to marry was given by the children's parents and specifically the parents of the bride. The right for a man and woman to marry is and always will be, a right given to us by our Heavenly Father.

It seems crazy to hear a pastor recite, "By the power vested in me by the state of 'take your pick,' I now pronounce you man and wife." What kind of "power" does the state even have?

What a bizarre statement to make. It would be more accurately stated, "By the power vested in me by the Living God of Abraham, Isaac and Jacob, I now pronounce you man and wife." Assuming, of course, that the couple desire to acknowledge the Living God in the first place.

Marriage has been *hijacked* by the government, plain and simple. Something that was once holy has now become reduced to nothing more than a secular contract with the state. The people of God need to return to the idea of holy matrimony and the sanctity of marriage, apart from the governmental system via the marriage license. Matrimony is specifically defined as man and woman joining together. Holy is something that is set apart. God's people need to become set apart from the 'world governing system' in place of Heaven's government.

Problems in Seeking Permission from the State

God created marriage, shouldn't the people of God give acknowledgement, where acknowledgement is due? The state marriage license gives no acknowledgement to God, whatsoever. He is not included in or even a thought in the license or certificate. The Word of God says, "fear the LORD and depart from evil." What does God think about the idea of a marriage license? Would He consider the marriage license evil? Evil is a strong word, no doubt about it.

"Evil" according to Merriam-Webster's Dictionary:

Evil[22]: "profoundly immoral and malevolent; harmful or tending to harm…"

So what does evil have to do with the marriage license? Again,

---

[22] Evil - By permission. From Merriam-Webster's Collegiate® Dictionary, 11th Edition ©2015 by Merriam-Webster, Inc. (www.Merriam-Webster.com)

why make agreement with an unholy, ungodly, immoral institution that condones unrighteousness such as baby killing (abortion), adultery, homosexual relationships, etc.? What is coming next? The legalization of incest and pedophilia? These things are completely evil, wicked and immoral. Throughout the Bible there is a common theme of God instructing His people to "come out from among them," "...friendship with the world is enmity with God..." and " in the world but not of it."

"License" according to Black's Law Dictionary:

License[23]: 1. A revocable permission to <u>commit some act that would otherwise be unlawful.</u> An agreement that it will be lawful for the licensee to enter the licensor's land <u>to do some act that would otherwise be illegal</u>, such as hunting game.

2. The certificate or document evidencing such permission.

Is God Right or is the State Right?

By signing a marriage license, a couple agrees with the idea that marrying someone of the opposite sex, is "criminal," but *"thankfully the state gave permission to do this illegal act, by granting them license to do so."* In all of history it has never been illegal for men and women to marry. Although, Bible readers know that it was prophesied in the book of 1 Timothy that in the last days humans would forbid marriage. The question is, does calling marriage an illegal activity mean the same thing as, "forbidding to marry?" Will the concept of marriage be completely erased from society all together?

1 Now the Spirit expressly says that in latter times some will depart from the faith, giving heed to deceiving spirits and doctrines of demons, ... 3

---

[23] License – By permission Black's Law Dictionary, 10th ed. 2014

forbidding to marry, and commanding to abstain from foods which God created to be received with thanksgiving by those who believe and know the truth. – (1 Timothy 4:1, 3 NKJV)

Why would Christians want to admit doing what God called good, criminal? Why sign off on something that is confirming something completely unbiblical? Again, it is not criminal to marry. When people sign the license document they are suggesting, "God you do not know what You are talking about. Marriage is not a good thing. Marriage is an illegal activity. We need to admit it is wrong, then get permission from the government for it to be legitimized and legalized. Otherwise without government permission, we are committing a crime." The idea of marriage being a crime without a license is completely false, untrue and absurd, especially for Bible-believers and followers of Jesus.

Double-Minded State

The state seems to have caught a severe case of double-mindedness. In the hour we live, the definition of marriage is under a significant level of scrutiny. Marriage is by definition an exclusive relationship between a man and a woman. Now, a small minority of people are attempting to hijack a definition that has been defined since the existence of time. For Christians and Jews, holy matrimony is at the core foundation of their doctrinal belief system. To erode the definition of marriage, is to erode the very foundation of a people's identity. While the government may flip flop and flop again on what that definition is, the believer in Jesus Christ of Nazareth, needs only hold onto what was defined back in the Garden of Eden.

The question needs to be asked in this hour, "If the state can take the ten commandments and prayer out of our school system, then why can't Christians, take their private marriage relationships out of the state?"

The state is swayed by the ever-changing moral compass of mankind's depravity. Christians specifically ought not to partner with the double-minded state. A house divided will not stand. Such a house is built on sand. When the storm comes, the house will collapse, because it was not built upon The Rock.

Fruit of Your Marriage

5 Trust in the LORD with all your heart, And lean not on your own understanding; 6 In all your ways acknowledge Him, And He shall direct your paths. 7 Do not be wise in your own eyes; Fear the LORD and depart from evil. 8 It will be health to your flesh, And strength to your bones. 9 Honor the LORD with your possessions, And with the firstfruits of all your increase; 10 So your barns will be filled with plenty, And your vats will overflow with new wine. – (Proverbs 3:5-10 NKJV)

This entire passage is applicable to marriage. Christians can trust the Lord with their marriage and family. He will direct families paths. Do not be wise in your own eyes (by signing the marriage license), but fear the Lord and depart from evil. In signing the license we are literally giving the fruit of the womb to the state. Departing from the evil of the license allows couples to unequivocally give their children to the LORD. He will strengthen you. He will cause your barns to overflow. Did you know that technically speaking the state owns your "property" and the "fruit of your marriage" which are your children? With a marriage license and birth certificate the children become "wards of the state."

Once children are born, the state becomes the legal guardian. People have gone to court battling for their children and have lost. *Parens patriae* is evident because the parents have signed these agreements stating one of the three incompetent options spelled out in a previous chapter.

The state becomes parent of the husband and wife. Do believers want God (YHWH) or the state, in the parental role, instructing couples how to function within the confines of marriage?

Parens Patriae Case Law

Believe it or not there is lawful precedence that prove this reality. The marriage license from a legal standpoint is in fact legal "ward" of your children. Maybe everything in you is refuting this notion? Technically speaking this is in fact what takes place when couples sign up for the marriage license contract. Signing rights away to the state to be the master of our marriages, owner of our children and yoked to an unholy institution propagating itself, as god and parent, again the idea of *parens patriae*. There is plenty of case law to support this evidence to be true and factual.

"Ex parte Wright, 225 Ala. 220, 222, 142 So. 672, 674 (1932). See also Fletcher v. Preston, 226 Ala. 665, 148 So. 137 (1933); and Striplin v. Ware, 36 Ala. 87 (1860). In other words, the state is the father and mother of the child and the natural parents are not entitled to custody, except upon the state's beneficent recognition that natural parents presumably will be the best of its citizens to delegate its custodial powers. See Chandler v. Whatley, 238 Ala. 206, 208, 189 So. 751, 753 (1939) (quoting Striplin v. Ware, 36 Ala. at 89) ("'The law devolves the custody of infant children upon their parents, not so much upon the ground of natural right in the latter, as because the interests of the children, and the good of the public, will, as a general rule, be thereby promoted.' ").'"

Ward[24]: – A person, usu. A minor, who is under a guardian's charge or protection.

Guardian[25]: – One who has the legal authority and duty to care for another's person or property, esp. because of the other's infancy, incapacity, or disability. A guardian may be appointed either for all purposes or for specific purposes.

The state is the undisclosed true parent. If the state does not like the way you are raising your children, Child Protective Services (CPS) can legally kidnap your children because of your marriage license and their birth certificate. By signing the marriage license, you give the state, which acts through CPS, power and authority over your children. Some people say, "They can take your kids away anyway, even without the marriage license, if they want." Yes, they can come and attempt to take your children away, legally, at least without signing the marriage license you are not giving them a leg to stand on. You will have more of a legal foundation to stand on without a marriage license, than you do with one.

All of this information is hidden from us and not communicated in a straightforward manner, intentionally. Who would agree to such terms and conditions knowingly? This is the level of ignorance and deception we have been lulled to sleep with, by the works of the evil one working through the

---

[24] Ward – By permission Black's Law Dictionary, 10th ed. 2014
[25] Guardian – By permission Black's Law Dictionary, 10th ed. 2014

state corporation. Satan does not play fair. He comes to deceive. He comes to bring bondage.

The Burglar Analogy

Signing a marriage license (and birth certificate included) is like going to sleep with the front door wide open. A burglar can simply walk in and take whatever they want at anytime. Without a marriage license and birth certificate, it would be similar to closing the front door and locking it. Yes, people can still get robbed, but at least the thief will have to work a little harder by picking a lock, kicking the door in, etc. Either way, anyone is susceptible to being robbed. The question is how much are people helping the burglar or preventing the burglar from stealing? Every couple will need to come to their own conclusion on this matter.

Corruption is everywhere. In varying degrees the government is corrupt in its legislation and verdicts. Thankfully, not every lawyer, judge, or jury is corrupt, but we do see injustice come forth in various ways. What else can people expect from a fallen world? Jesus is the only one who can bring perfect justice, which He will, at the end of the age. Believers in Jesus Christ are waking up to the problems of agreement with the state through covenant contracts such as marriage licenses, birth certificates, and other programs of dependence.

Political Agenda Against the Christian Family

Republican or Democrat, it does not matter. They are all on the same team. The plan is well established. Listen to what one of our state officials said in a radio interview, Senator Peter Hoagland in 1983:

"Fundamental, Bible-believing people do not have the right to indoctrinate their children in their religious beliefs because we, the state, are preparing them for the year 2000, when America will be part of a one-world global society, and their children will not fit in."

This is why the Bible says, "You are not of this world." Praise the Lord for not fitting into this one-world global society, that wants to erase the Word of God.

"Karl Marx said that in order to establish a perfect socialist state, you have to destroy the family." Quoted by family psychologist and author John Rosemond. "You have to substitute the government and its authority for parental authority in the rearing of children."[26]

These two quotes greatly oppose the Word of God. Moreover, these thoughts and ideas undermine the foundation upon which this nation was created.

State License Terms & Conditions

All the states are relatively the same in their statutes regarding the marriage license. Every state should have the statutes (terms and conditions) for marriage license available on their respective governmental website. Most states, if not all, do not offer a printed copy of the terms and conditions with the state marriage license application. This generally means people do not think or know there are any terms and conditions to the marriage contract, they are about to find themselves involved in.

The State of Ohio's Terms & Conditions

Looking at one particular state, Ohio has several problems in their legislation to be aware of. Please see verbiage taken

[26] Does your child belong to the state? http://www.wnd.com/2011/11/372409/

straight off the website below:

"Marriage is a legal, as well, as a spiritual and personal relationship. When you state your marriage vows, you enter into a legal contract. There are three parties to that legal contract: 1) you; 2) your spouse; and 3) the state of Ohio. The state is a party to the contract because under its laws, you have certain obligations and responsibilities to each other, to any children you may have, and to the state of Ohio.[27]"

Notice, in the terms and conditions of the contract, the husband and wife are in fact "married to the state" contractually speaking. <u>The state has complete and total jurisdiction over the marriage, because of the marriage license contract signed by the couple.</u> The couple must comply with all laws established by the government pertaining to their marital relationship without any say. The marriage is instantly and permanently a creature of the state. Included in the terms and conditions as mentioned before is the fact the state also has jurisdiction over the fruit and property of the marriage.

Interesting to note, the state of Ohio defines marriage with three distinct relationships:

1. Legal

2. Personal

3. Spiritual

The evidence of the legal relationship, is the contract. The personal relationships created are between the husband, wife and the state of Ohio. What about the spiritual relationship? Is

---

[27]https://www.ohiobar.org/ForPublic/Resources/LawFactsPamphlets/Pages/LawFactsPamphlet-35.aspx

God or anything spiritual mentioned? It seems quite clear, it is non-existent, unless, the state of Ohio sees itself as a god. That would account for the relationship being spiritual, where the husband and wife worship the state by granting it all authority over the marriage. The state grants permission to marry creating the terms and conditions of the contract. They control the entire nature of the legal relationship. When the officiate says, "By the 'power' vested in me by the state of Ohio I now pronounce you husband and wife," the spiritual element is exposed. The state has set itself up as a god. The God of the Bible is nowhere to be found or mentioned in the agreement.

What about this relationship is spiritual, if the husband and wife are atheist or agnostic? Is it possible for something to be "spiritual" for two people, who do not believe in God to begin with? The point is, the state, would be the one making this a spiritual reality in some convoluted way. Such an idea falls right in line with Karl Marx' plan for socialism.

Notice that in the verbiage quoted it says, "1) you; 2) your spouse; and 3) the state of Ohio." The state does not even define the marriage from a male, female standpoint - husband and wife. They have already set up their legal structure and vocabulary for the doorway of "any" kind of creature-based relationship. It is not legal today for anything other than male and female matrimony to be recognized in Ohio (as of April, 2015). The groundwork is already laid, if a day were to arise, where the laws change towards permitting other ungodly defined relationships.

Where is "licensing" taking us?

- What if down the road, everyone with a marriage license is limited to a particular number of children?

- What if the state forces people to become sterilized, kill babies or some other practice invading an individual's privacy?

- What if the government begins attempting to license parenthood?

These are absurd thoughts, because everyone has the God-given right to have children and it is perfectly legal under the United States Constitution. Yet, that is exactly what is going on right now with marriage! The control is escalating day by day. If the state changes the terms and conditions of the agreement, the nuclear family could begin to look even more skewed from God's original design. We the people are on a slippery slope regarding the legalities of marriage and family in the United States of America. The law shapes the constructs of what family looks like with significant implications. Should we continue in this direction as a nation or even as individuals? I hope not.

A Word from Hosea

1 Hear the word of the LORD, You children of Israel, For the LORD brings a charge against the inhabitants of the land: "There is no truth or mercy Or knowledge of God in the land. 2 By swearing and lying, Killing and stealing and committing adultery, They break all restraint, With bloodshed upon bloodshed. 3 Therefore the land will mourn; And everyone who dwells there will waste away With the beasts of the field And the birds of the air; Even the fish of the sea will be taken away. 4 "Now let no man contend, or rebuke another; For your people are like those who contend with the priest. 5 Therefore you shall stumble in the day; The prophet also shall stumble with you in the night; And I will destroy your mother.

6 My people are destroyed for lack of knowledge. Because you have rejected knowledge, I also will reject you from being priest for Me; Because you have forgotten the law of your God, I also will forget your children. 7 "The more they increased, The more they sinned against Me; I will change their glory into shame. 8 They eat up the sin of My people; They set their heart on their iniquity. 9 And it shall be: like people, like priest. So I will punish them for their ways, And reward them for their deeds. 10 For they shall eat, but not have enough; They shall commit harlotry, but not increase; Because they have ceased obeying the LORD. - (Hosea 4:1-10 NKJV)

Prayer

Father, may we not be the people Hosea speaks about. Turn our hearts away from blind ignorance. Let the laws, statutes and precepts of this nation be established upon righteousness. Let Your justice pour out from Heaven. Let the lies and deception flowing from all world governmental systems stop right now in Jesus name. Turn our hearts toward the things that matter to You. Let us see the folly and error of our ways, so as to turn from them. Expose the ignorance and let the Truth connect to our hearts. Let us not be wise in our own eyes. Cast down the gross pride and arrogance of this nation. Let us be a people that seek to walk in humility, rather than by being humbled because of how we take pride in sinning before You. May we be a people that move into righteousness, holiness, and justice for the Living God according to Your ways. Holy Spirit, I ask that You bring revelation and light to this topic. I ask You to speak to the hearts of Your people, so the bold Truth will rise and everything else be burned. Let Your Word speak. May the Holy Spirit of God give us, His people, greater revelation as to how to walk the earth in this hour. How to stand against an unrighteous governing body that is in direct opposition to the things of a Holy God. May we enter into the sufferings of

Christ according to righteousness.

Father, thank You that You are strong enough to save us, Your children. In Y'shua's (Jesus') name. Thank You.

Then the Lord answered me and said: Write the vision And make it plain on tablets, That he may run who reads it. (Habakkuk 2:2 NKJV)

13

ADHESION CONTRACT

What kind of contract is the marriage license? The marriage license is an adhesion contract. Well, what does that mean? Take a closer look at Black Law's Dictionary.

Adhesion Contract[28]:

"A standard-form contract prepared by one party, to be signed by the party in a weaker position, usu. A consumer, who has little choice about the terms. – Also termed contract of adhesion; adhesory contract; adhesionary contract; take-it-or-leave-it contract; leonine contract."

Adhesion Contract - For a contract to be treated as a contract of adhesion, it must be presented on a standard form on a "take it or leave it" basis, and give one party no ability to negotiate because of their unequal position. Notice how the definition uses the word, "consumer." This word choice lends itself to the idea that the state is a corporation "selling" a product or service

---

[28] Adhesion Contract – By permission Black's Law Dictionary, 10th ed. 2014

to a "consumer." The state clearly has a primary focus of control tied to revenue generation, simply by offering such a contract to begin with.

Some examples of everyday adhesion contracts would be the following:

Social Security Card/Numbers

Driver's Licenses

Birth Certificates

Cell Phone Contracts

Cable TV Contracts

Online User Agreements

The list goes on, but you get an idea as to how one identifies the adhesion contract. All of these contracts are on a voluntary basis.

Taking a Closer Look at the State Marriage License

The state marriage license is in fact a 3-way secular adhesion contract (or covenant) between you, your spouse and the state. The state is the principal in your secular marriage contract. The husband and wife are secondary parties; subject to whatever the state legislates as law without any say.

This document is dynamic and subject to change at the whims of the state. The husband and wife have no voice or argument in the matter. Rarely, if ever, are couples provided the terms and conditions regarding the "voluntary" state marriage license. Most people are not aware these terms and conditions even exist. The state completely fails to communicate or offer these terms and conditions in writing, when providing the state license itself.

One could argue this is not a true contract. A contract must be entered into knowingly, understandably, intentionally and fully informed. Without such knowledge, understanding and aptitude, technically there can be no contract. I refer to such actions as "designed ignorance" on the state's part. Apparently, there are no "lemon" laws when dealing with the state's "sales" integrity or lack thereof. Ignorance is a huge asset to any sales process. The less the customer knows, the more likely the company with a sales proposition will close the sales transaction in their favor. What makes matters worse is the fact the state keeps the employees ignorant as well. After calling several states and speaking with countless people, it is clear – ignorance is the plan. Nobody can give a straight answer. The state benefits in keeping both their employees and the unsuspecting couple in the dark as to the details of this contract. Remember back to the meeting in 1911, where the state's goal was to <u>"abolish common law marriage."</u> Achieving this goal means revenue generation year after year via the fees associated with the state license, not to mention bigger revenues on the back end through divorce. The state cannot make any money off of a "common law" or "biblical" marriage.

When the couple provides payment for the licensing fee, "consideration" takes place, communicating the establishment of a covenant. Signing and paying for a license, instantly establishes agreement between the three parties. All of the state's statutes, rules and regulations instantly become active in this relationship.

Are you beginning to notice the similarities of government and business? It is time to shift our thinking of government. Government has become a business, rather than an institution seeking the good of the people, as it was originally intended to be. The nation was founded on the idea of a "government for the people by the people," but now there is much more at play in our government's motivation.

In researching the definition of the adhesion contract and reviewing court law, there is one document that really "nails the hammer on the head" regarding the "business proposition" of the marriage license. This document is called, "Challenging Adhesion Contracts in California: A *Consumer's* Guide." The entire document is about defining what kind of contracts businesses can present to consumers. The adhesion contract makes it possible for "business" to take place. Businesses add all kinds of terms and conditions so as to give themselves the advantage against any harm or responsibility for wrongdoing towards the consumer. The document is quite revealing as to how corrupt businesses can become because the consumer signs off on the particular service contract. The biggest problem with the government adhesion contract is that no one is holding it accountable to prevent them from taking advantage of citizens. Aside from God, it does not appear that there is any other agency watching to ensure justice for the people.

Look at the Terms and Conditions

As much as Christians want to tell themselves God is a part of the state marriage license covenant, He is not. He has zero, zilch, nothing, to do with this "voluntary" adhesion contract. God is not considered, mentioned or welcomed in any capacity. He is not named anywhere in the terms, conditions or paperwork. Here are some questions that need to be asked pertaining to marriage and the state's involvement:

- Since when did marriage become a business proposition with a state institution?
- Isn't marriage simply about defining a private "relational status" between two people?
- How can God be a part of any contract that He is not even mentioned in?

What can be done about these realities?

14

THE FRAUD MATTER

As previously discussed, marriage and family, are one of the most important elements of any society. God established humanity through the sanctity of marriage. Without man and woman coming together in the confines of marriage, civilization would completely fail to exist, as God intended. The holy union of man and woman was one of the first blessings God gave to humanity.

In this country, marriage is clearly under attack on all sides. In fact, broken marriages are a global issue. This is not new information. The news, movies, TV shows, music, all communicate this fact loud and clear. The question is, "Why is this happening?" Part of the reason is because the government is making laws and regulations promoting the degradation of marriage and beyond that, the family unit. Another reason is that the government has attempted to replace God in every sense.

The United States of America, founded upon Christian principles, leads the world in the amount of divorces that take place every single year. Yes, the United States of America is number 1, when it comes to the divorce rate. On top of that, Wikipedia says that 60-76% of Americans claim to be Christian.[29] So what is going on in the church?! These are sobering statistics.

Christians who are "born again" and seeking the Kingdom of God and His righteousness, ought not experience the pain of divorce. So why are they? There are a number of areas we can look to because it is a complex issue. I mention the stats on divorce, not to condemn those who have experienced such painful loss, but to point out the issue. Why is it so tough for marriages to stay together today? There has got to be more going on here than meets the eye! It was not always like this, as we look at the words of Jesus.

Jesus said to them, "Moses, because of the hardness of your hearts, permitted you to divorce your wives, but from the beginning it was not so. – (Matthew 19:8 NKJV)

What are couples participating in that they "believe" are righteous acts, but are really not? Such a question is a huge can of worms. For the purposes of this book, let's focus on the "voluntary" marriage license. Is the government committing fraud against its citizens, by concealing or misrepresenting the truth? Now, you might be saying to yourself, "Wow! Those are strong words. Fraud? Really? I do not know that I believe that…"

Fraud[30]:1. A knowing misrepresentation or knowing

---

[29] https://en.wikipedia.org/wiki/Christianity_in_the_United_States
[30] Fraud – By permission Black's Law Dictionary, 10th ed. 2014

concealment of a material fact made to induce another to act to his or her detriment. Fraud is usu. a tort, but in some cases (esp. when the conduct is willful) it may be a crime. — Also termed intentional fraud.

2. A reckless misrepresentation made without justified belief in its truth to induce another person to act.

3. A tort arising from a knowing or reckless misrepresentation or concealment of material fact made to induce another to act to his or her detriment. • Additional elements in a claim for fraud may include reasonable reliance on the misrepresentation and damages resulting from this reliance.

4. Unconscionable dealing; esp., in contract law, the unfair use of the power arising out of the parties' relative positions and resulting in an unconscionable bargain. See defraud. — fraudulent, adj.

Illinois Website on Marriage License

Here is one example taking place against the American people. Illinois' website has the following statement:

"Before getting married in Chicago or suburban Cook County, couples must obtain a marriage license from the Cook County Clerk's office.[31]"

Merriam-Webster's definition of "must"

Must[32]: 1 *a* : be commanded or requested to <you *must* stop> *b* : be urged to : ought by all means to <you *must* read that book>

2: be compelled by physical necessity to <one *must* eat to live> : be required by immediate or future need or purpose to <we

---

[31] http://www.cookcountyclerk.com/vitalrecords/marriagelicenses/Pages/default.aspx
[32] Must - By permission. From Merriam-Webster's Collegiate® Dictionary, 11th Edition ©2015 by Merriam-Webster, Inc. (www.Merriam-Webster.com).

must hurry to catch the bus>

3*a* : be obliged to : be compelled by social considerations to <I *must* say you're looking well> b : <u>be required by law, custom, or moral conscience to</u> <we *must* obey the rules>   *c* : be determined to <if you *must* go at least wait for me> d : be unreasonably or perversely compelled to <why *must* you argue>

4: be logically inferred or supposed to <it *must* be time>

5: be compelled by fate or by natural law to <what *must* be will be>

6: was or were presumably certain to : was or were bound to <if he did it she *must* have known>

7*dial* : <u>may, shall —used chiefly in questions</u>

Here is where things get a little sticky. Notice how there are multiple meanings and definitions for one word. How do we know which one to use? The definitions of words are how a society is able to accurately and justly give out court rulings. <u>In the Black's Law Dictionary the word "must" is defined under the definition of "may." The word "must" does not have its own listing in Black's Law dictionary.</u>

The lawyers are veiling the true intention or realities of the people's rights. While the common individual thinks of the Merriam-Webster definition "required by law" perspective, the legal definition is what is important. The word "may" is also interchangeably used with the word "must." So what seems like fraud from the outset based upon common law, has become a matter of semantics and definition of choice. The lawyers know full-well how to ride the razors edge in this game of cat and mouse. We the people need to become educated, rightly, so as to avoid this game all together. All of this, wording and definitions are used in a shrewd manner so the state corporation can "close the sale" and generate revenue again and again.

In regards to the Illinois website, the word, "may" can be interchanged with the word "must." The slight difference is quite substantial because "may" is optional in our thinking, while "must" comes across as mandatory. All of this wording is used to prod people into the marriage license adhesion contract.

Illinois Case Law

The following Illinois case law, goes so far as to use the word "require." Take a close look at some rulings from the state of Illinois.

"When two people decide to get married, they are required to first procure a license from the state. If they have children of this marriage, they are required by the state to submit their children to certain things, such as school attendance and vaccinations.

Furthermore, if at some time in the future the couple decides the marriage is not working, they must petition the state for a divorce. Marriage is a three-party contract between the man, the woman, and the state. Linneman v. Linneman, 1 Ill.App.2d 48, 50, 116 N.E.2d 182, 183 (1953),citing Van Koten v. Van Koten, 323 Ill. 323, 326, 154 N.E. 146 (1926).

The state represents the public interest in the institution of marriage. Linneman, 1 Ill.App.2d at 50, 116 N.E.2d at 183. This public interest is what allows the state to intervene in certain situations to protect the interests of members of the family. *The state is like a silent partner in the family* who is not active in the everyday running of the family but becomes active and *exercises its power and authority only when necessary* to protect some important interest of family life. Taking all of this into consideration, the question no longer is whether the state has an interest or place in disputes such as the one at bar, but it becomes a question of timing and necessity. Has the state intervened too early or perhaps intervened where no intervention was warranted? This question then directs our discussion to an analysis of the provision of the Act that allows the challenged state intervention (750 ILCS 5/607(b) (West 1996))."[33]

The state of Illinois is fervently attempting to "require" a marriage license. It is illegal for Illinois to "require" anyone to sign a marriage license according to the U.S. Constitution and the ruling of the Supreme Court Meister vs. Moore in 1877. By the definition of "fraud," the state of Illinois is committing fraud by making this declaration. Plain and simple, the people have been deceived at the state level regarding the issue of the marriage license.

Now, if a couple DOES apply for a state marriage license, they are in fact "required" to follow the obligations of the agreement, in regards to their children.

Look at the U.S. Supreme Court Ruling

96 U.S. 76 - 24 L.Ed. 826 MEISTER v. MOORE October, 1877

"No doubt, a statute may take away a common-law right; but there is always a presumption that the legislature has no such intention, unless it be plainly expressed. A statute may declare that no marriages shall be valid unless they are solemnized in a prescribed manner; but such an enactment is a very different thing from a law requiring all marriages to be entered into in the presence of a magistrate or a clergyman, or that it be preceded by a license, or publication of banns, or be attested by witnesses. *Such formal provisions may be construed as merely directory,*

---

[33] See more at:
http://caselaw.findlaw.com/il-court-of-appeals/1486817.html#sthash.4KofxrrT.dpuf

instead of being treated as destructive of a common-law right to form the marriage relation by words of present assent. And such, we think, has been the rule generally adopted in construing statutes regulating marriage."[34]

Defining "Directory" according to The Law Dictionary.org:

Directory[35]: A provision in a statute, rule of procedure, or the like, is said to be directory when it is to be considered as a *mere direction or instruction of no obligatory force,* and involving no invalidating consequence for its disregard, as opposed to an imperative or mandatory provision, which must be followed. The general rule is that the prescriptions of a statute relating to the performance of a public duty are so far directory that, though neglect of them may be punishable, yet it does not affect the validity of the acts done under them, as in the case of a statute requiring an officer to prepare and deliver a document to another officer on or before a certain day.

Essentially, the state wants the people to believe we "must" (from the Merriam-Webster definition - required by law) apply for or obtain a state marriage license and certificate, while hiding behind (Black's Law definition - may) the Federal Court system ruled the license is "merely directory." If people want to "voluntarily" sign this piece of paper from the state to have their marriage "recognized" then they may do so. Not having signed any such paper from any state is quite alright, assuming some fundamental principles are followed to "prove" your marriage. This topic will be discussed further in a later chapter.

Over the years, the state government has become very good at propagating the supposed requirement of a state issued marriage license and certificate. Nothing could be further from the truth. The United States Constitution is founded upon common-law principles that can only be surrendered at the "consent" or

---

[34] https://supreme.justia.com/cases/federal/us/96/76/case.html
[35] Directory: http://thelawdictionary.org/directory/

"volunteering" of the individual. Matrimony is a contract and relational status of an adult man and woman. The state does not have any business being involved, unless otherwise invited.

15

LAWS OF THE LAND

As discussed in previous chapters, the marriage license is completely "voluntary." *No one is being forced to sign the license.* The government cannot make a couple register their marriage. People choose to do this voluntarily.

The United States Constitution

Now what about obeying the laws and ordinances of the land? Yes! Absolutely, let's follow the authority of the land. The 1st amendment of the Constitution of the United States of America reads:

"Congress shall make no law respecting an establishment of religion, or prohibiting the free exercise thereof; or abridging the freedom of speech, or of the press; or the right of the people peaceably to assemble, and to petition the Government for a redress of grievances."[36]

---

[36] http://www.billofrightsinstitute.org/founding-documents/bill-of-rights/

Freedom to Practice Religion

1 Let every soul be subject to the governing authorities. For there is no authority except from God, and the authorities that exist are appointed by God. 2 Therefore whoever resists the authority resists the ordinance of God, and those who resist will bring judgment on themselves. 3 For rulers are not a terror to good works, but to evil. Do you want to be unafraid of the authority? Do what is good, and you will have praise from the same. 4 For he is God's minister to you for good. But if you do evil, be afraid; for he does not bear the sword in vain; for he is God's minister, an avenger to execute wrath on him who practices evil. – (Romans 13:1-4 NKJV)

The founders of this Republic (the United States of America) put the Word of God above any and all of man's laws. In fact, the laws of the land were subject to the Bible first and foremost because of the 1st amendment right in the United States Constitution.

When a couple signs a marriage license they "give up" their God-given right in exchange for a "privilege" from the state. Keep in mind, a privilege can be revoked or changed at any point. A "right" is unshakeable. The people are well-served in holding onto their God given rights!

What is also noteworthy is the idea that the absolute legal authority of the United States of America is the Constitution. The President, Congress and Supreme Court are all subject to this authority - the law of the land. The first amendment of the Constitution is the idea of "freedom of religion and freedom of speech." If the religious doctrine I follow, indicates that I can be married without a marriage license, then in a very real sense of the law, I can be legally married with a valid, lawful marriage.

It is time to take a stand. Please say, "NO" to the marriage license. Let's give our marriages back to God.

The U.S. Supreme Court Defines "Liberty"

"In 1923 the U.S. Supreme Court defined "liberty" as the right to, "marry, establish a home and bring up children…"

MEYER vs. STATE OF NEBRASKA, 262 U.S. 390 (1923)

'No state … shall deprive any person of life, liberty or property without due process of law.'

"While this court has not attempted to define with exactness the liberty thus guaranteed, the term has received much consideration and some of the included things have been definitely stated. Without doubt, it denotes not merely freedom from bodily restraint but also the right of the individual to contract, to engage in any of the common occupations of life, to acquire useful knowledge, to marry, establish a home and bring up children, to worship God according to the dictates of his own conscience, and generally to enjoy those privileges long recognized at common law as essential to the orderly pursuit of happiness by free men."[37]

For those reading this, that currently have a marriage license or have had one in the past, take hope. Remember James 4:6, stay in a place of peace, because "He gives more grace." Chances are you did not question any of this and did not know the ramifications of the marriage license. *There is a deliberate deception taking place towards the people.* Fortunately, people are now beginning to stand against unrighteous tyranny.

Make no mistake, mankind is under attack by the evil one. The government is just one tool he uses to kill, steal and destroy.

Be sober, be vigilant; because your adversary the devil walks about like a roaring lion, seeking whom he may devour. (1 Peter 5:8 NKJV)

---

[37] https://supreme.justia.com/cases/federal/us/262/390/case.html

Licenses are Designed to Deny People

The reason *any* license throughout history has been instituted was so that the power of "denial" could exist. In the mid-1800s, if a county or state didn't want interracial marriages, they could simply deny the license. If whites and blacks did not obtain a marriage license, further consequence could ensue. Eventually in 1923, the "Uniform Marriage and Marriage License Act" was passed by the federal government – 6 years later, marriage licenses were being distributed in every state to all people, including interracial couples. Marriage had now become a government institution. Prior to this act, most marriages other than interracial ones, never included a license. Marriage throughout the world was and is a fundamental right.

Declaration of Independence in Congress, July 4, 1776

Here is an excerpt from the Declaration of Independence.

"The unanimous declaration of the thirteen United States of America. "We hold these truths to be self-evident, that all men are created equal, that they are endowed by their Creator with certain inalienable Rights, that among these are Life, Liberty and the pursuit of Happiness.---"[38]

Our government began with the idea of freedom. Every man has inalienable rights and marriage is one of those rights.

Human life comes about righteously when an adult male and adult female come together in holy matrimony. Men and women have the freedom and right to be lawfully married without permission or contract from a state institution. For Bible believers, marriage is between God, the man and the woman. How is holy matrimony to take place within a state institution that denies the very existence of a Creator?

It is highly advisable not to be yoked with the state, in a

---

[38] http://www.archives.gov/exhibits/charters/declaration_transcript.html

covenant so vital as marriage. Somehow people have become blinded to this reality. All too often Christian couples partake in the state license. Thankfully, the Church is waking up. Can holy matrimony truly exist if the state is a silent partner in the marriage? Jesus did not redeem the state, die for the state or have any part in the state government's covenant – i.e. license. His government and this world government function separate from one another. It is time to discern between the holy and unholy, the clean and unclean. May God's people exit the world drowning in delusion, to find refuge in the "ark" of His covenant.

16

SOLUTIONS FOR A LEGAL MARRIAGE, WITHOUT A MARRIAGE LICENSE

One of the big questions to address in this book is: Can a man and woman be legally married in the USA without a state marriage license? Whether people realize it or not, from a legal standpoint, there are multiple options that exist for a couple to define their marriage relationship. In today's culture, the most practiced option is the state issued marriage license and certificate, which falls under civil law. Any other form of marriage outside civil law, would fall under common law. Every marriage in the Bible has been defined in common law and practiced long before the marriage license existed. States have worked hard to cover up and sweep common law marriage under the rug. It is very much a legitimate option, where people today in 2015, can enter into holy matrimony without the state.

Common Law Marriage

The concept of marriage simply communicates a change in relational status. Common law helps determine which people are husband and wife, and which people are involved in another type of a relationship outside the confines of marriage. How does society know conclusively who is married and who is not? For varying reasons it is important to identify the marriage relationship. As an example, if there is an unfortunate death, who will inherit the property from the individual who has passed away? What if there is a medical emergency and only the family can see the individual in the hospital? Defining the relationship openly helps bring forth the necessary evidence for situations that may need to be addressed.

The only time it is required for the law to get involved regarding a marriage, is in the case where the validity of the relationship is in question. Using prior case law, helps to determine the relational status in question, and whether or not a marriage was truly established. As in the example of a spouse passing away, it is necessary to determine if the couple was married before the death occurred.

Common Law[39]: The body of law derived from judicial decisions, rather than from statutes or constitutions.

The courts look to previous examples to determine how to identify what marriage is and is not.

The US Supreme Court ruling of Meister vs. Moore in 1877, highlighted two realities:

---

[39] Common Law – By permission Black's Law Dictionary, 10th ed. 2014

1. Marriage is a common right.

2. A marriage license is merely directory (or in other words voluntary.)

<u>Common law marriage is lawful and legal.</u> The popular misconception of "common law marriage" is that people tend to think it is not legal, when in fact it is totally 100% legal. Common law marriage is not "recognized" by all of the states, but it is legal in all 50 states. Let that sink in for a moment. Read it out loud a couple of times and meditate on what is being communicated. Americans have been indoctrinated so much, that it can take multiple times reading this material for the truth to take hold. (See the end of the chapter to see which states "recognize" common law marriage.)

Statutory or (Civil) Law[40]: 2. The body of law imposed by the state, as opposed to moral law. 3. The law of civil or private rights, as opposed to criminal law or administrative law.

Directory Requirement[41]: A statutory or contractual instruction to act in a way that is advisable, but not absolutely essential — in contrast to a mandatory requirement. A directory requirement is frequently introduced by the word should or, less frequently, shall (which is more typically a mandatory word).

As discussed, the issue is not whether common law marriage is "legal" it is simply a question as to whether or not it is "recognized" by a particular state. The reason it is not recognized is because the state has nothing to do with the contract of common law marriage. Since the state is "left out" of the covenant/contract completely, they do not know

---

[40] Statutory – By permission Black's Law Dictionary, 10th ed. 2014
[41] Directory Requirement – By permission Black's Law Dictionary, 10th ed. 2014

anything about the "terms and conditions" and are not even a party to the contract. Thus it is not recognized by the state. The same way God is left out of the state license covenant, the state is left out of the biblical or common law covenant. Understand, there is a distinct difference between "unlawful" and "recognized." God's people need to identify and discern the differences between the two ideas.

"Civil or statutory marriage" is registered with the state and includes a three-party adhesion agreement between state, the husband and the wife or a three-party agreement between the state and two homosexuals. The state is part of this marriage license contract, therefore they keep track of these records. Due to the fact that the state is part of the "civil or statutory marriage," there are terms and conditions the state must provide each couple. When couples sign such an agreement, the state then can recognize and record that relationship.

Any marriage not "recognized" by the state, does not automatically mean it would be an "invalid or illegal" marriage. Common law marriage, is legal and valid in every state. It simply may not be "recognized" by every state in the union, simply because the terms and conditions are unknown to the state. The state is not part of the covenant, contract, agreement, etc.

Identifying Common Law Marriage

What does the court use to identify the validity of a marriage? The court uses jurisprudence, in other words, previous case law. There are specific questions the court may ask couples to prove their marriage.

Some of these questions may include:

Is there any kind of contract - oral or written?

Verbal agreements do stand up in a court of law to validate a marriage. However, if one spouse dies, then proving the verbal agreement, outside of witnesses, could be difficult. It is highly advisable to develop a written agreement signed by both husband and wife. The family Bible can also be signed as a legal marriage contract valid in a court of law, which was commonly practiced less than a hundred years ago.

Is there a marriage contract presently or one written for the future?

One might be wondering what a future marriage agreement is? There are some couples who have written an agreement to marry at a particular future date. In some cases the court has ruled the relationship a marriage. Although this is not common, it has been known to happen. Keep in mind, even though courts have supported future tense marriage, such an agreement is by no means as secure as a present tense contract. Such marriage contracts are best written to communicate the fundamental rights and duties of the parties involved.

Has a wedding ceremony or solemnization taken place?

A religious wedding ceremony is no longer necessary to the court when determining and identifying a marriage. The reason for this is due to the fact that agnostics and atheists would not be seen as having a valid marriage. These groups may still have a ceremony; it need not be "religious" in nature for the wedding and marriage to be established in a court of law.

Did any religious figure perform the ceremony?

While it is an indicator that a "wedding" took place, it is not necessary to have someone perform a ceremony in order for the couple to be seen as married. Adam and Eve and Isaac and Rebecca are two examples that highlight this reality. The only individual responsible for performing a ceremony in those cases would have been God Himself.

Were there witnesses to the ceremony or solemnization?

This element is helpful in creating the argument for a valid marriage. It is public and has witnesses to verify that a wedding took place and a marriage was formed. Remember, a ceremony simply offers more credibility to the evidence of a marital relationship being established.

Has cohabitation taken place?

Consummation and cohabitation play a role in the evidence of a marriage being established. Isaac and Rebecca basically met and then went into his mother's tent to consummate the marriage. From that point on, the two were married and Isaac loved his wife. The court system takes this relational element into account.

Did the couple make a marriage certificate to solemnize the day their marriage began?

A certificate of marriage can be created on your own. Hire someone to make one or simply use the family Bible. Fill out the certificate with dates, names, and even the location the wedding or agreement took place. Have the certificate signed by the husband and wife, along with three other witnesses such as the pastor and a couple of family members. Ultimately, the signature of three other witnesses will communicate the agreement of the husband and wife's marital status.

Was there a secret marriage?

Sometimes it is necessary for a couple to have a "secret" marriage. In such cases, the court has ruled these type of marriages, valid and legal. Secret marriages are more challenging to prove and therefore it is advisable to make the marriage relationship public.

Are there any previous marriages in place prior to the marriage in question?

The court, in most cases, will not recognize a relationship as a marriage, if there is a pre-existing marriage in place. Before a couple can get married, any previous marriages must be dissolved through the court system properly and legally. If both parties have never been married before then there is no issue to be concerned with on this point.

Is the marriage based on false information?

If two people join together and one person has falsified their identity, the validity of the marriage could very well be in question. The court will deal with such issues case-by-case.

Investigating the Relationship

The judicial system generally looks at the overall scope of the couple's relationship, with key elements to be identified as defining marriage or not. If you are sincere in your intentions to marry, make it as plain as day for anybody to look at your relationship and say, "Of course they are married." Obviously, there are varying needs and circumstances as to how or why people portray themselves in a certain light. Simply attempt to follow some of the guiding fundamentals and you will be all right.

Items That Help Prove Any Marriage

Over the course of time, marriages have been determined, lawful, based upon certain key elements that may verify the relationship. This is a list of markers that the court can use as evidence to determine a marriage relationship exists:

- Parental Consent
- Public Notice in Newspaper announcing the Wedding
- Wedding Ceremony – A public traditional wedding ceremony is very helpful in proving the common law marriage, although it is not necessary to have a religious figure officiate the wedding.
- Wedding Guest Book - Conveys a list of people who can testify to solemnization.
- Marriage Contract - Verbal or written agreement by the male and female.
- Certificate of Marriage - Signed by officiate, husband, wife, and two other witnesses. A document of this kind is in fact considered a legal record, which makes the common law marriage both legal and lawful. This document could be registered, as well, with the County Clerk or Registrar. With a certified copy of the original notice, this could be presented as if it were a marriage license.
- Memorialize the Wedding - With pictures and video documentation.
- Cohabitation - Once verbal or written agreements are signed and you are officially married, begin cohabitating together.

- Public Reference - Refer to one another as husband and wife.

The purpose of this chapter is to lay out legal options for those hoping to marry without direct government involvement. For those concerned about what Romans 13 and 1 Peter speak to regarding obeying authorities, your conscience can be clear on all counts.

Marriage Examples in the Bible, are Common Law

Adam and Eve, Isaac and Rebekah, Jacob and Rachel are all biblical marriages that demonstrate common law marriage. Common law marriage provides honest, sincere Christians a real viable marriage option. Is it less popular today, than a marriage license? Yes. Any less valid? No. This is not an unlawful approach to justify any type of sin (as many think in today's culture). Individual men and women are legally able to marry, without being yoked to the government through adhesion contract of a state license.

The Word of God is holy. God is looking for a people set apart to Him. Common law is biblical and for believers should promote a greater level of commitment, with God's favor and blessing. A biblical common law marriage must be taken seriously, joyfully, and deserves real attention. The covenant of marriage lasts a lifetime.

Reasons for Proving Marriage

A couple may have to prove the validity of their marriage, to receive rights or benefits unavailable to singles. Some examples of this are life insurance, medical benefits, death benefits, etc. Generally speaking, if a business is asking for proof of marriage, a notarized or properly executed marriage certificate ought to suffice. In the event such evidence is unsatisfactory, a sworn affidavit ought to work out. The only time the affidavit will not work, is when the opposing party rebuts the affidavit.

If a government agency, challenges the validity of your marriage, submit the marriage certificate. If any particular business or corporation is not satisfied with the marriage certificate, ask for an "administrative hearing."

Should a hearing be required, some tips to follow:

- Provide evidence of marriage agreement, certificate and memorialized evidence such as guest book, pictures, and/or video of the wedding.

- Testify about the reality of your marriage: Prove you are living together, that you have children together, refer to each other as husband and wife. Site the Meister vs. Moore case that state marriage licenses are merely directory in nature. There cannot be any adverse consequence or invalidation for not following a statute which is only directory.

- Ask the agency representative (who should not be the hearing officer) to be sworn in. Then ask him or her to enter into the official record any evidence the agency possesses "invalidating" your common law marriage.

Show up prepared, and chances are likely the court will rule in your favor. If not, you can take it to an appeals court and provide the same evidence where the court will eventually rule in favor of your marriage.

What About Fake and False Marriage Arrangements?

In a fallen world, with sinful humanity, there is going to be corruption. Marriage is no exception to this reality. Occasionally people claim to be married, that are not. This can happen with a state marriage license (statutory marriage) or a biblical marriage (judicial law). An example of this is when people pretend to be married to gain citizenship in a particular country. A foreigner, paying a United States citizen a sum of money to become a citizen through "marriage," happens fairly regularly. Human nature is predisposed to abusing laws and common law marriage is no exception.

People will continue to misrepresent themselves and the truth of a relationship. It should be no surprise that this behavior will continue until heaven and earth pass away. The judicial system has established guideposts to accurately determine the validity of a marriage.

People who are genuinely interested in establishing a life-long committed marriage, are well-served in using their right to "common law" and biblical matrimony. Marriage is holy in the eyes of God, must be handled with reverence, remain undefiled and something where two people are set apart unto each other, the rest of their life.

In the Event of Divorce Under Common Law

Every marriage is centered on an agreement or contract, whether it is common law or statutory law.

In dealing with such matters there are two options:

1. Go to the statutory court and subject your marriage to their rules and regulations. The court is not concerned about taking people's time, money or telling them how

to run their family business. As soon as a couple places their marriage and family under the court's jurisdiction, they are under the court's control. No questions asked, no rebuttals. It is their way or the highway. Also, keep in mind, the children and the property become the state's once they come under their body of law. This is mentioned and discussed in prior chapters.

2. Write out a covenant before marriage. Communicate each other's roles, wishes, desires and expectations for marriage. Depending on the couple, some find value in writing out what would happen if one desired to end the relationship. This statement is true, "If you love me, you will put it in writing." Loving someone means looking out for his or her best interests. Putting expectations on the table, in written form, helps increase understanding for the couple.

A significant reason couples choose common law marriage is so they can be adults determining the nature of their private, personal relationship. The state has no business butting in on the couple or family, unless invited.[42]

States "Recognizing" Common Law Marriage

This is a list of states that currently "recognize" common law marriage, as of December 2014. Remember, "recognize" and "lawful" are two different things. Common law marriage is "lawful" and "legal" in all fifty states.

- Alabama, Colorado, District of Columbia, Georgia (if created before 1/1/97), Idaho (if created before 1/1/96), Iowa, Kansas, Montana, New Hampshire (for inheritance purposes only), New Mexico, Ohio (if created before 10/10/91), Oklahoma (Oklahoma's laws and court decisions may be in

---

[42] http://www.originalintent.org/edu/marriage.php

conflict about whether common law marriages formed in that state after 11/1/98 will be recognized.), Pennsylvania (if created before 1/1/05), Rhode Island, South Carolina, Texas, Utah

17

HOW CAN I GET OUT?

How can a couple get out of the marriage license relationship with the state?

There are at least two possible options regarding leaving the state marriage license:

1. A couple can take the state to court for not providing the terms and conditions of the marriage license. According to contract law, there cannot be a valid signature, if the signee had not been provided full disclosure when the agreement was presented. The terms and conditions should be provided to any individual in conjunction with the contract. If a couple was not provided such information, then the contract can be voided, because there was not proper consideration before signing. Talk with a contract lawyer regarding options as to voiding the marriage license.

2. Visit the family court and "divorce the state." Communicate to the court the intention of divorcing and dissolving the relationship legally. The overall idea for the couple is to keep the marriage together in the eyes of God

and each other, restructuring the relationship from a legal standpoint. To the state, the couple would appear to be divorced. After that, have a marriage ceremony without the marriage license, in front of friends, family, or witnesses. Even if the ceremony is only in front of a few people, have it anyway. In a court of law, the couple will be able to prove a marriage exists, after the recent ceremony.

This book is in no way giving legal advice or legal counsel as to how any individual or couple is to proceed in this issue of the marriage license. Each couple needs to determine what is best for their relationship and that it is advised individuals speak with a lawyer. There are so many dynamics that can take place. Only the married couple would be able to determine the best route, with the idea of dissolving the contract with the state. To suggest divorcing the state, has profound implications. Things to consider are the unity of the marriage, the health of the marriage, and any children under age 18 which may cause additional challenges in the court system. Ultimately, as Christians, become educated on the legalities, read the Word of God, pray about it and respond to what the Holy Spirit reveals.

If there are dependent children involved, consider waiting until they are age 18, before divorcing the state. Otherwise, the family could come under the state's statutes in family court. The state will define the parameters for visitation, etc. The time to test the waters for divorcing the state, are ideal before having children or after all children are 18 years old. Again, these are simply suggestions and things to be aware of.

Whatever the solution or direction a couple proceeds in, unity is key. Please seek counsel to best determine solutions that may specifically work for you.

Depending on which state a couple lives in, things will play out uniquely to that body of law. The reader is encouraged to research and investigate the matter with proper counsel and due diligence. Each state has a website with statutes for the marriage license and also the dissolution process.

Implications of the State Marriage License

As government and society remove a Holy God from public life, Bible-believing Christians can expect obstacles, trials and challenges. The government is legislating more and more wickedness, which is in direct opposition to the Living God. Maintaining marriage, while being yoked to the state, in this three-party contract is an unnecessary burden. As the government redefines marriage terms and conditions, there will be a direct affect on Christian heterosexual marriages. All of this takes place in the spiritual realm first and then in the physical realm.

The power of "agreement" in the spiritual realm is everything. The demonic can influence any believer in Jesus Christ, just as easily as a non-believer. Bondage comes about through agreement in any form with the demonic realm. These forms of agreement – come in the spoken word, the written word or belief systems. Because the government is attempting to redefine marriage legally, current marriages established through the marriage license are directly affected by these changes.

Participating in inner healing ministry for over ten years, I have seen first hand what the power of agreement does to keep an individual in bondage. It is only when the individual comes out of agreement with a particular lie, does their freedom come forth. One example comes to mind. A girl came to receive ministry, repeatedly, for depression. Nobody knew how to address this problem. When she finally asked the Holy Spirit where the lie came in, she was able to get free. Apparently, her uncle said something to her at the age of ten and she agreed with it. She agreed with the lie at a young age. The girl renounced the lie and the depression instantly lifted. She left with a smile on her face. We never saw her again, praise Jesus! Similarly, the state license agreement affects marriages adversely, because of the immoral statutes and law legislated. People and marriages can still function agreeing with a certain lie. The point is that God has more for us and we can experience greater freedom, tangible and intangible, without such agreements.

23 And the word of the LORD came to me, saying, 24 "Son of man, say to her: 'You are a land that is not cleansed or rained on in the day of indignation.'

25 "The conspiracy of her prophets in her midst is like a roaring lion tearing the prey; they have devoured people; they have taken treasure and precious things; they have made many widows in her midst.

26 "Her priests have violated My law and profaned My holy things; they have not distinguished between the holy and unholy, nor have they made known the difference between the unclean and the clean; and they have hidden their eyes from My Sabbaths, so that I am profaned among them. (Ezekiel 22:23-26 NKJV)

God's people are beginning to distinguish between the holy and unholy, the clean and unclean with increasing measure.

No Condemnation

1 There is therefore now no condemnation to those who are in Christ Jesus, who do not walk according to the flesh, but according to the Spirit. (Romans 8:1 NKJV)

A Word from James

4 Adulterers and adulteresses! Do you not know that friendship with the world is enmity with God? Whoever therefore wants to be a friend of the world makes himself an enemy of God. 5 Or do you think that the Scripture says in vain, "The Spirit who dwells in us yearns jealously"? 6 But He gives more grace. Therefore He says: "God resists the proud, But gives grace to the humble." 7 Therefore submit to God. Resist the devil and he will flee from you. 8 Draw near to God and He will draw near to you.

Cleanse your hands, you sinners; and purify your hearts, you double-minded. 9 Lament and mourn and weep! Let your laughter be turned to mourning and your joy to gloom. 10 Humble yourselves in the sight of the Lord, and He will lift you up. – (James 4:4-10 NKJV)

The book of James is packed with so much intense goodness. The author gets right to the point. James 4:4 hits it on the head. Our nation is filled with adultery, in and out of the Church. The physical reality of adultery taking place in this country, is a parallel to what is taking place in the spiritual realm. The Church has become friends with the world. There are too many agreements with this world system. What does adultery in our relationship with the Living God look like? If we seek the face of God, individually and collectively, as His people, He will begin to reveal the truth.

The Holy Spirit wants us. The Church compromises by embracing the world system over the King of Heaven. God is jealous for us as individuals, families, communities, and nations. He exhorts followers of Jesus to cast down idols and not make graven images on earth, heaven or sea below.

4 "You shall not make for yourself a carved image--any likeness of anything that is in heaven above, or that is in the earth beneath, or that is in the water under the earth; 5 you shall not bow down to them nor serve them. For I, the LORD your God, am a jealous God, visiting the iniquity of the fathers upon the children to the third and fourth generations of those who hate Me, 6 but showing mercy to thousands, to those who love Me and keep My commandments. (Exodus 20:4-6 NKJV)

Anything put before God is considered an idol. The Word of God is a lamp unto our feet… as Psalm 119 communicates.

James continues to expound upon the goodness of God, "He gives more grace." Believers commit adultery with God by loving the things of this world. He extends even more grace when we do turn to false gods, committing adultery against Him. He is so good! Worthy is the Lamb that was slain! James expresses how to respond. In one word, "REPENT." Said another way, "change your mind." Humanity can all too often become double minded and prideful. It is time for the Church to cleanse their hearts and hands. The Word of God needs to define the believer's perspective, not the other way around.

Prayer

Father in Heaven, I thank You that You hear our prayers. Thank You for Your amazing grace! Thank You for helping us by the power of Your Holy Spirit, to return to our first love - You. Help us to walk faithfully, rightly dividing the Word of God with truth and righteousness. Help us to discern the clean from the unclean. Help us to walk humbly, love mercy and do justly in all our being. Let wisdom come upon Your marriages. Let wisdom come upon singles considering marriage. Let hunger for Your perfect will come forth in might and power in profound measure like the world has never seen. Let wisdom and discernment come forth for those seeking dissolution from the state. Bring forth the right questions and answers each couple needs to address, to rightly align their marriage relationship. I ask that You surround these couples with righteous counsel. I ask for Your warring and ministering angels to encamp about Your people prayerfully considering what to do with this information. Place a fiery hedge of protection around them. Thank You for endowing Your Church in humility, meekness and faithfulness in the days coming forth. Heal marriages Lord, every broken marriage that needs Your touch. I ask for great grace and rich mercy to pour out on all families in the earth right now. Do a radical work of transformation in the hearts of man, to love You first and then love their neighbor as their self. Come Holy Spirit and breathe afresh on Your people. In Y'shua's mighty name. Amen.

18

VOWS, ADULTERY
& DIVORCE

Some people might make the argument that common law
marriage is used when two people are not sincere in their
commitment to one another. Frankly, for true followers of
Jesus, nothing could be further from the truth. Marriage is a
very real, holy, sacred commitment and professing believers
need to grasp this reality. This chapter will explore the Word of
God and gain Jesus' perspective surrounding the marriage
covenant.

Marriage from the Perspective of Two Believers

This chapter is written with a focus toward followers of Jesus,
those who desire to sincerely approach marriage from God's
perspective, will and purposes. Those individuals who would
confess, "Jesus is my LORD, Master and Savior." Additionally,
this would include people who are looking to enter holy
matrimony for the first time or those who have been widowed.

Secondarily, this chapter might be of interest to those believers who are married, divorced, remarried and those considering remarriage. For this audience, interpreting scripture accurately for their personal situation, will need to be addressed, on a case-by-case and situation-by-situation basis. Understanding the topic of divorce and remarriage deserves the utmost respect and consideration in regards to righteous living in the sight of Jesus Christ. This chapter is not focused at unbelievers or relationships where one individual is a believer and the other is not.

God cares deeply about the marriage commitment. Wise decisions made today, can help prevent people from experiencing pain later. Thankfully, regardless of good or bad choices through true repentance, there is mercy, grace and love offered to overcome any situation.

The hope of this chapter is to increase value and respect for the marriage relationship. Marriage is a big deal. Please understand, with or without the marriage license, the purpose of marriage is to stay together until the end. No one should go into marriage with one foot in and the other foot out. Wavering as to whether or not one intends to stay committed, pure and faithful is what Jesus would call "foolish," according to Matthew 7:26. This chapter is written in the context of the Sermon on the Mount – Matthew 5-7.

Jesus raises the standard in Matthew 5 and calls His Church to operate from a higher place through the empowerment of the Holy Spirit. By the death of Jesus on the cross and His resurrection, the baptism of the Holy Spirit empowers God's people with grace, to walk as Jesus walked. The same Spirit that raised Jesus from the dead, is now in the born again baptized believer. With that being said, keep in mind that love is sacrificial – this means giving something up for another. Love is not an emotional infatuation that feels good for a moment and when the moment's over, walk away from it. That is selfish and narcissistic, the opposite of love.

In God's eyes, there is a call to "die" for the sake of another, when united with a spouse. Jesus says, "It's because of your hardness of heart that Moses permitted a certificate of divorce, but in the beginning it was not so."

Three topics Jesus focuses on surrounding marriage are: vows, adultery and divorce. Marriage is the biggest commitment made between two people. The idea here is to fully capture God's heart for the respect and appreciation He has for the covenant relationship between husband and wife.

Vows

What are followers of Jesus aiming for? Take time to meditate and dialogue with the Holy Spirit as you read Psalm 15. It is rich with virtue.

1 A psalm of David. LORD, who may dwell in your sacred tent? Who may live on your holy mountain?

2 The one whose walk is blameless, who does what is righteous, who speaks the truth from their heart;

3 whose tongue utters no slander, who does no wrong to a neighbor, and casts no slur on others;

4 who despises a vile person but honors those who fear the LORD; who keeps an oath even when it hurts, and does not change their mind;

5 who lends money to the poor without interest; who does not accept a bribe against the innocent. Whoever does these things will never be shaken. (Psalm 15:1-5 NIV)

This psalm is an amazing invitation from the Lord. The psalmist lays out the characteristics of what it takes to dwell in God's sacred tent and live on God's holy mountain. Focus on verse 4, in regards to this chapter. Are God's people going to "keep their oath/s even when it hurts, and not change their mind?" What would it look like to truly walk in the fear of the LORD? Keeping oaths, vows and promises might then become more possible, perhaps, even easier.

The righteous response in a marital commitment is to stick it out, no matter how challenging or bad the circumstances seem. For two self-proclaimed followers of Jesus, walking away from marriage, outside of sexual immorality, is sin. Even then, divorce is not Jesus' heart for marriage. His desire is for the couple to remain together. Keep in mind, separation may be a necessary option for a season of time. One spouse may need to deal with issues that make it unsafe for the other spouse to live under the same roof. This is not divorce, but simply waiting upon the LORD to bring salvation and healing to an area where the enemy has attacked and caused wounding.

People cannot blame anyone for their spousal decision. Making a seemingly poor choice, is their responsibility. Nobody holds a gun to someone's head forcing them into marriage. Standing before the Most High God and a group of people, committing devotion to another for the rest of their life, is something to follow through on. Running away from the commitment is not the answer. Saying, "Oops, I made a mistake. I did not realize they had alcohol issues, debt issues, physical abuse issues, sexual issues, anger, immaturity, laziness, addictions, depression, etc." This is the point of dating and the engagement process to really understand who this other person is you are going to marry. Sadly, it is really too late after the fact. There is no turning back. The good news is that nothing is too far-gone for the healing touch and deliverance from the Most High God. He makes all things beautiful in His time.

Psalm 15 talks about fulfilling obligations, even at one's own expense. Divorce is shortsighted, this side of eternity. Keeping our eyes focused on eternity, makes the follow-through on marriage worthwhile. Gary Thomas's book "Sacred Marriage" is a great read, that develops this idea of keeping eternity in mind throughout your marriage. This book expounds upon the true nature of marriage, not Hollywood's depiction. One example that Thomas uses in the book, is that of Abraham Lincoln. He was arguably the best President this nation has ever seen, while his wife was arguably the worst first lady. Thomas tells the story of how Lincoln's marriage to his wife was used to fortify his character to withstand the challenges of his call as President of the United States of America. This perspective of God's purpose for marriage is both sobering and inspiring.

Divorce exposes the reality that our love is weak and faithless to believe God's Word. God is capable of making all things new. He is big and well-equipped to handle the most challenging circumstances. Believe that Jesus is capable of working things out, "for the good of those who are called according to His purpose."

Jesus brings clarification to oaths in Matthew 5:

33 "Again, you have heard that it was said to the people long ago, <u>'Do not break your oath, but fulfill to the Lord the vows you have made.'</u> 34 But I tell you, do not swear an oath at all: either by heaven, for it is God's throne; 35 or by the earth, for it is his footstool; or by Jerusalem, for it is the city of the Great King. 36 And do not swear by your head, for you cannot make even one hair white or black. 37 <u>All you need to say is simply 'Yes' or 'No'; anything beyond this comes from the evil one.</u>

(Matthew 5:33-37 NKJV)

Highlighting Jesus' statement above:

1. Generally when attending a wedding, vows are recited by the bride and groom. Before Jesus' time vows (oaths) were unto God and were to be fulfilled, whatever they might be – pertaining to marriage or some other commitment. Even though the couple is speaking to one another, the vows (oaths) are to be fulfilled unto the LORD.

2. Jesus warns and commands the people to not make oaths or vows at all. The text actually suggests to cut vows out of the wedding ceremony all together because anything more than a "Yes" or "No" is from the evil one. The people of God do not need to make vows to each other, but simply keep the things they say "Yes" or "No" to.

Generally, people enjoy verbalizing their vows in the wedding ceremony because without vows, what is left to the ceremony?

How do people get married? Aren't vows mandatory to qualify a marriage relationship? Not at all, as we have already discovered in previous chapters.

It seems worthwhile to simply change the wording up a little. What if the husband and wife did this?

Example:

John Doe and Jane Smith want to marry.

John – "I take you Jane Smith as my wife. Will you take me John Doe as your husband?"

Jane – "Yes. I do. I Jane Smith take you John Doe to be my husband. Will you take me Jane Smith as your wife?"

John – "Yes. I do."

This is a verbal agreement, preferably done in front of witnesses.

Something else a couple might want to communicate is their "desire" to love, serve, and enjoy their spouse as they move forward into marriage. These do not need to be vows, but simply a confession of the vision they have for their role in the marriage. Be creative in this element of the ceremony, making it personal and meaningful. Keep in mind, communicating "desires" or something similar, again is not mandatory.

Adultery

Let's explore what some of the Scriptures say regarding "adultery."

- *"You shall not commit adultery. (Exodus 20:14 NKJV)*
- *'The man who commits adultery with another man's wife, he who*

commits adultery with his neighbor's wife, the adulterer and the adulteress, shall surely be put to death. (Leviticus 20:10 NKJV)

- *'You shall not commit adultery. (Deuteronomy 5:18 NKJV)*

- *Whoever commits adultery with a woman lacks understanding; He who does so destroys his own soul. (Proverbs 6:32 NKJV)*

- *All of Jeremiah 3 – you will need to look this one up.*

- *14 Also I have seen a horrible thing in the prophets of Jerusalem: They commit adultery and walk in lies; They also strengthen the hands of evildoers, So that no one turns back from his wickedness. All of them are like Sodom to Me, And her inhabitants like Gomorrah. 15 "Therefore thus says the LORD of hosts concerning the prophets: 'Behold, I will feed them with wormwood, And make them drink the water of gall; For from the prophets of Jerusalem Profaneness has gone out into all the land.' " (Jeremiah 23:14-15 NKJV)*

- *"For they have committed adultery, and blood is on their hands. They have committed adultery with their idols, and even sacrificed their sons whom they bore to Me, passing them through the fire, to devour them. (Ezekiel 23:37 NKJV)*

- *All of Hosea 4 – you will need to look this one up.*

- *27 "You have heard that it was said to those of old, 'You shall not commit adultery.' 28 "But I say to you that whoever looks at a woman to lust for her has already committed adultery with her in his heart. 29 "If your right eye causes you to sin, pluck it out and cast it from you; for it is more profitable for you that one of your members perish, than for your whole body to be cast into hell. 30 "And if your right hand causes you to sin, cut it off and cast it from you; for it is more profitable for you that one of your members perish, than for your whole body to be cast into hell. (Matthew 5:27-30 NKJV)*

- *20 "Nevertheless I have a few things against you, because you allow that woman Jezebel, who calls herself a prophetess, to teach and seduce My servants to commit sexual immorality and eat things sacrificed to idols. 21 "And I gave her time to repent of her sexual immorality, and she did not repent. 22 "Indeed I will cast her into a sickbed, and those who commit adultery with her into great tribulation, unless they repent of their deeds. 23 "I will kill her children with death, and all the churches shall know that I am He who searches the minds and hearts. And I will give to each one of you according to your works. (Revelation 2:20-23 NKJV)*

Several important points communicated in these passages:

1. Do not commit adultery.
2. If an individual commits adultery, they are instantly put to death, under the old covenant.
3. If an individual commits adultery, they lack understanding and destroy their own soul.
4. Adulterer's likened to Sodom and Gomorrah, eat wormwood, drink gall and profaneness has gone out into all the land.
5. Pagans do such practices.
6. Jesus raises the standard and makes adultery an issue of the heart, not just the outward act. When an individual looks with lust they are in danger of being cast into hell.
7. Jesus will throw Jezebel on a sickbed. Those who commit adultery with Jezebel will go into the great tribulation, unless they repent. Jesus will kill her children.

Jesus Christ is quite serious about the issue of adultery because it is so harmful to the individual. The fruit of adultery causes separation between husband and wife and also separation from God. God deeply loves people. He is the Good Shepherd who wants to protect His sheep. He is communicating the extreme danger for those who participate in the sin of adultery. For individuals who believe and make the confession that Jesus is their LORD, Savior and Master, they are poorly served to dismiss the sin of adultery. It is a very big deal to the heart of God.

Looking with Lust

If your right eye causes you to sin, pluck it out and cast it from you; for it is more profitable for you that one of your members perish, than for your whole body to be cast into hell. (Matthew 5:29 NKJV)

According to Jesus, looking at an individual with lust in their eyes is committing adultery. The danger is real, eternal separation from God! Watching pornography is lusting, thereby committing adultery, subjecting the individual to the possibility of being cast directly into hell! Hell! The Lake of Fire! How much worse is hell, than simply dying, as was the punishment in the Old Covenant? Let this reality sink in. Meditate on Jesus' words regarding this matter.

"And do not fear those who kill the body but cannot kill the soul. But rather <u>fear Him who is able to destroy both soul and body in hell.</u> (Matthew 10:28 NKJV)

The Church needs to stop justifying actions in place of God's Word and Spirit. Just because other people are making poor decisions outside the Word of God and call themselves Christians, does not justify our actions before the LORD. I am tremendously convicted right now and sense the weighty "fear of the LORD" over this subject. This is a major problem and issue of concern. Please do not gloss over the warnings and exhortation of Jesus in this conversation. The Author of Life, is warning about His judgment, and ultimately hell fire.

Who, but Jesus really knows how great His mercy is? How great is His grace? How narrow is the narrow path? How few are the few who find it? These are some difficult questions. What side do we want to err on?

A Word from James and Paul

4 Adulterers and adulteresses! Do you not know that friendship with the world is enmity with God? Whoever therefore wants to be a friend of the world makes himself an enemy of God. 5 Or do you think that the Scripture says in vain, "The Spirit who dwells in us yearns jealously"? 6 But He gives more grace. Therefore He says: "God resists the proud, But gives grace to the humble." (James 4:4-6 NKJV)

"I say then: Walk in the Spirit, and you shall not fulfill the lust of the flesh." (Galatians 5:16 NKJV)

God's Word is sure and true. Why not press into fullness of purity? The Holy Spirit is the Helper who enables us to no longer participate in such practices. Holy Spirit's presence, empowers believers to overcome the things of the flesh. The believer rejoices in the mercy and grace of Jesus and for their name to be written in the Lamb's Book of Life. Participating in sin, specifically the sin of adultery, will reap death in some form, for believer and unbeliever alike.

For the wages of sin is death, but the gift of God is eternal life in Christ Jesus our Lord. (Romans 6:23 NKJV)

Prayer

Father in Heaven, I repent for all the ways in which I have been guilty of committing adultery in my heart. Bring Your light to the areas of my heart needing Your change, healing and purity. Have mercy on me LORD. Thank You for forgiving me. Have mercy on us as a people and grant us the gift of true repentance. Holy Spirit I invite Your truth to come and change me. I lift up the inhabitants of the earth, LORD, and ask that You cast down the adulterous, lustful spirit. Let all people turn from this wickedness and unrighteousness. Let there be a return to righteousness and purity. Moreover, let Your children love purity and seek righteousness in great measure. Let Your people walk with hearts after You, hating unrighteousness. In the mighty name of Jesus Christ of Nazareth. Amen. Thank You LORD.

In closing out this section of adultery, look at one last scripture discussing this topic.

Stoning the Woman in Adultery

3 Then the scribes and Pharisees brought to Him a woman caught in adultery. And when they had set her in the midst, 4 they said to Him, "Teacher, this woman was caught in adultery, in the very act. 5 "Now Moses, in the law, commanded us that such should be stoned. But what do You say?" 6 This they said, testing Him, that they might have something of which to accuse Him. But Jesus stooped down and wrote on the ground with His finger, as though He did not hear. 7 So when they continued asking Him, He raised Himself up and said to them, "He who is without sin among you, let him throw a stone at her first." 8 And again He stooped down and wrote on the ground. 9 Then those who heard it, being convicted by their conscience, went out one by one, beginning with the oldest even to the last. And Jesus was left alone, and the woman standing in the midst. 10 When Jesus had raised Himself up and saw no one but the woman, He said to her, "Woman, where are those accusers of yours? Has no one condemned you?" 11 She said, "No one, Lord." And Jesus said to her, "Neither do I condemn you; go and sin no more." - (John 8:3-11 NKJV)

- Where is the man who was caught in the act of adultery with the woman? It takes two to commit adultery (from a physical standpoint), so whom were the Pharisees failing to bring accusation upon? There is already a level of hypocrisy taking place on behalf of the Pharisees by leaving out the other party.

- Their test was flawed. Jesus knew this full-well. A true test would bring both adulterer and adulteress forward, according to the law in Leviticus 20:10.

- Their own sin is exposed. The deceitfulness of their hypocrisy is revealed in their protection of the male. Both male and female should have become subject to the judgment of stoning. The Pharisees showed mercy and grace to the man by not exposing him, but condemnation to the woman.

- What was Jesus writing in the dirt? There is much speculation as to what He was writing. One idea is that He was writing the ten commandments or possibly a scripture verse like Leviticus 20:10. Reminding the hypocrites that they too are sinners, along with the man they failed to put on trial.

- Jesus demonstrated compassion, mercy and grace towards this adulterous woman. He protected her from the fullness of the law, as the Pharisees protected their colleague, friend or relative from the fullness of the law.

- Jesus fully hates sin, yet fully loves people. He is zealous for humanity. He wants people to experience the abundant life. There are significant consequences when people take part in any kind of sin, adultery included. When Jesus says, "...go and sin no more," I believe this woman repented and never committed the sin of adultery again.

- In today's culture people do not get stoned for committing adultery, but the cost is potentially greater. The implications affect one's soul and emotions. Living with this trauma, over a lifetime, could potentially be a worse punishment than being stoned immediately. We, as a people, need a healthy dose of the fear of the

LORD, while receiving His tremendous mercy and grace. The responsibility for individuals is to confess and repent sin. He is faithful and just to forgive and wash away condemnation and shame. Jesus demonstrates mercy and grace, not only for the adulterous woman, but also for all the people who were around Him. He could have risen up and judged all the people perfectly. Jesus exemplified compassion on all those who were present in this setting. He knew all of their sins and condemned no one directly.

When Two Believers Divorce

31 "Furthermore it has been said, 'Whoever divorces his wife, let him give her a certificate of divorce.' 32 "But I say to you that whoever divorces his wife for any reason except sexual immorality causes her to commit adultery; and whoever marries a woman who is divorced commits adultery. (Matthew 5:31-32 NKJV)

- If she commits sexual immorality, then she is already an adulteress, correct? It seems divorce makes the divorcee an adulteress.

- Divorcing a wife for any reason outside of sexual immorality causes her to commit adultery. Anyone who marries the divorced woman commits adultery as well.

3 The Pharisees also came to Him, testing Him, and saying to Him, "Is it lawful for a man to divorce his wife for just any reason?" 4 And He answered and said to them, "Have you not read that He who made them at the beginning 'made them male and female,' 5 "and said, 'For this reason a man shall leave his father and mother and be joined to his wife, and the two shall become one flesh'? 6 "So then, they are no longer two but one flesh. Therefore what God has joined together, let not man separate." 7 They said to Him, "Why then did Moses command to give a certificate of divorce, and to put her away?" 8 He said to them, "Moses, because of the hardness of *your hearts, permitted you to divorce your wives, <u>but from the beginning it was not so.</u> 9 "And I say to you, whoever divorces his wife, except for sexual immorality, and marries another, commits adultery; and whoever marries her who is divorced commits adultery." 10 His disciples said to Him, "If such is the case of the man with his wife, it is better not to marry." (Matthew 19:3-10 NKJV)*

- In verse 6, Jesus says when two come together in marriage, let no man separate. The understanding here is that under no circumstance may anyone separate a couple.

- The Pharisees understood what He was saying, which went against the idea of a "man" issuing a certificate of divorce. This would be a separation, going against Jesus' words in verse 6. They bring up the question about Moses in verse 7. It is the hardness of heart, a lack of love that allowed for a divorce certificate to be issued.

- Notice verse 9, if a man divorces his wife (for any other reason besides sexual immorality) and remarries another woman, he commits adultery. Agree or not, I read this as, "if a man divorces a woman for any reason other than sexual immorality and gets remarried, he is committing '<u>ongoing adultery.</u>'"

Jesus points out in the book of Mark that the issue of adultery is a two-way street. Men are just as guilty as women. There is no double-standard in His eyes.

11 So He said to them, "Whoever divorces his wife and marries another commits adultery against her. 12 "And if a woman divorces her husband and marries another, she commits adultery." (Mark 10:11-12 NKJV)

Adultery, by definition, is having sex with someone other than one's spouse. Please look up the definition. Jesus is saying, this form of "remarriage," is simply defined as adultery, not something sanctified with His blessing. He is communicating that for the married couple that divorces, remarriage is committing adultery. Any marital or sexual relationship after divorce, is invalid (unless the spouse has died). The two options for the original couple is reconciliation or celibacy. The original marriage covenant is what Jesus identifies as holy matrimony and sanctified in His eyes. He does not validate this second marriage, in any capacity, throughout scripture. He only identifies it as adultery.

Clarifying the matter at hand, the man marrying the divorced woman, commits "ongoing adultery." If the original couple divorces and both remarry, there is a total of four people committing "ongoing adultery." Jesus only permits divorce to those who have committed adultery. With that being said, He does NOT indicate the individual is free to "remarry."

Here is why the term, "ongoing adultery" is used. Jesus calls the spouse that remarries, an adulterer. When does adultery come into the equation? When the two become "married." What happens when two people marry? They have sex. Jesus calls this adultery. Does that mean the first time they have sex is adultery and thereafter it is no longer adultery? Why would it? If it were adultery the first time the couple has sex, wouldn't the case be true for the 50th, 100th, 1000th time etc.? Jesus never indicates a timetable for when the adultery ends. He simply communicates that the two in question - commit adultery.

Options for Two Believers Regarding Divorce

There are three options for a couple (who going into marriage) considered themselves followers of Jesus and divorce:

    1.   Divorce, never get married again and live a life of celibacy.

2.   Wait until the divorced spouse dies. Death is the only thing that breaks the covenant of marriage in God's eyes. Once this occurs, the remaining spouse is free to remarry.

3.   The previously married couple change their mind about the divorce and reconcile. They humble themselves before God and each other, to unite again.

Sadly, culture and Hollywood's message, have completely destroyed the sacred and holy dynamic God intended for marriage. Commonly, couples marry, live together for a while and when they are not happy or personally gratified, they walk away. How often do movie stars set an example of marrying 2, 3, 4, 5 times, not to mention all the sexual immorality that takes place in-between marriages? Society begins to believe and accept this lie as normal life, as if it is okay to join in with this depravity. People who claim to be followers of Jesus are to rise to the standard of Jesus Christ Himself, in the power of the Holy Spirit. There is grace to rise up, because God has poured out His Spirit upon us.

Generally speaking, the Church has room to grow in keeping their commitments and word. All too often double-mindedness creeps in. Now is the time to confess sin and "change our mind" according to righteousness as stated in the Bible. What if the Church could stop doing what is right in its own eyes? Love and marriage are not always easy. Marriage requires two people focused on Jesus. Couples need integrity, character, and sacrificial love in order to make it to the end - faithful, holy and pure. Leaning into God and His Word makes this possible.

He came as a Lamb the first time. He is coming as a Lion the second time. Jesus will bring justice upon all wickedness and will judge it righteously.

Prayer

Father God, thank You for Your Word of truth. Let us become a people after Your heart, after Your Word and led by Your Holy Spirit. Help us to be single-minded, to count the cost and to persevere to the end. Let us be a people of self-control. Thank You that Your Holy Spirit empowers us to walk as Jesus walked, rising to His standard. Help us to take up our cross and follow Your example Jesus. Let Your light come forth in great power. Thank You that Your love covers a multitude of sins. We love You Jesus. In Your name. Amen.

To Those Divorced and Possibly Remarried

This chapter has been directed at those followers of Jesus, who are single, have never been married or widowed, and are considering marriage. For those reading this book that have been married before, desire to remarry or are already remarried, seek the Lord's answer in His Word. For the purposes of this book, exploring "all" the possible scenarios of remarriage, will not be possible. Search it out and do not take anyone's word for what is acceptable for your situation. This is totally between you, God and His Word – The Bible.

Some scenarios for remarriage might include:

- Husband and wife were not Christians when they got married. They divorced and then later one became a Christian remarrying someone else.

- Two unsaved people get married. One spouse gets saved, eventually the unsaved spouse abandons the other, even though the saved spouse is working to stay together. Please see 1 Corinthians 7.

Again, please seek out the Lord on this matter by reading His Word. Consider talking with different credible sources for counsel regarding your particular circumstances.

The Words of Jesus are real, gracious and filled with truth. How are believers going to walk this out in light of His Words? Jesus says, "If you love Me, then obey my commands." The wages of sin is death. Any time people, saved or unsaved, participate in sin, the promise of death exists in one form or another. Let the Holy Spirit speak through the Words of Jesus. His conviction and truth are gracious and right. Everyone will stand before the perfect One, individually for his or her actions. One Man's thoughts are all that matter on the Day of Judgment. How people choose to walk their lives out now, will affect them for all eternity. Some of you will have to make some very hard, painful decisions. I know that in light of eternity it will be worth it. This life is temporary, eternity is forever.

One shot is all there is at this thing called life. There are no second chances, once the flesh falls limp. All of humanity falls short of the glory of God. The beauty of the Cross of Calvary is for those who confess Jesus Christ as LORD and Savior, the blood of Jesus covers *all* sin, aside from the blasphemy of the Holy Spirit. The awesome reality of being a Christian is the complete recognition of mankind's desperate need for a Savior in Christ Jesus. We do not aim to continue in sin, but to respect the blood that was shed - which defeated sin and death. Obeying Jesus' commands is evidence of love towards Him. Love Him. Love Him well. He is worthy! Peace be with you.

19

THE HOMOSEXUAL
STATE LICENSE

There is a battle taking place at the federal and state level, regarding the issue of homosexuality. The government is passing new laws this year (2015), allowing the legalization of homosexual relationships. From a biblical perspective, such relationships are not equal or similar to that of heterosexual marriage. "Marriage" is, and always will be, an exclusive relationship between one man and one woman. It has been this way throughout all of human history.

According to the Bible, the God of Abraham, Isaac and Jacob, does not acknowledge "homosexual union" in any legal capacity and this union is simply defined as sin. Scripture defines such activity as "abominable and lawless." Our nation's government and the Government of Heaven, do not see eye-to-eye on this topic. State and federal government no longer have a clear definition, understanding or appreciation for marriage – one man and one woman in a legal committed relationship.

In a day when marriage and the family unit is under attack from all sides, followers of Jesus Christ need to ask, why? Why are marriages and families, in the body of Christ, falling apart at unprecedented rates? Remember what Karl Marx stated, "In order to have a perfect socialistic society, you have to destroy the family unit." This is exactly what the government is legislating, condoning and advocating.

Reflect on these simple realities…

- This world's government system is losing sight of righteousness on all counts, in this case specifically marriage and family.

- Bible believers know homosexual acts have nothing to do with marriage. These acts are unrighteous, unholy and illegal in the sight of a Holy God.

- A "license" is the permission to do something that would otherwise be illegal.

- It has never been illegal for a man and woman to marry in YHWH's eyes or mankind's eyes for that matter.

The time has come for the people of YHWH to change the way the game is played…

- Stop voluntarily signing the marriage license covenant with the state. Signing this document communicates your belief that for a man and woman to marry, it is a criminal act, that is illegal and requires permission from an unholy governmental system.

- If the government thinks it is a good idea to license homosexual acts, then by definition, a license is perfectly fitting. Man's wisdom is clearly on display in this conversation and it is a pathetic argument.

Governments condoning sexual perversion will only invoke the judgment of the Most High God. A perfect example of this is Sodom and Gomorrah, cities that were destroyed due to sexual perversion. YHWH's people need to separate out from this world governing system.

Bible-believers need to stand against such wicked laws coming to fruition. This is the hour to stand for righteousness. Pray, fast and take action – people's souls and eternal well-being are at stake! With that being said, there are Bible-believing men and women at work within the governmental system. However, the government as a whole, is not submitted to Jesus Christ or the Word of God, and this is the major problem. Pray for the government officials, legislation and for godly men and women to take office. Pray they will not compromise under the pressure of corruption.

Homosexual Acts

Homosexual acts are an abomination before the eyes of the Creator, "illegal" and "unlawful" according to the Word of God.

'If a man lies with a male as he lies with a woman, both of them have committed an abomination. They shall surely be put to death. Their blood shall be upon them. (Leviticus 20:13 NKJV)

Abomination[43]: something abominable: extreme disgust and hatred: loathing.

24 Therefore God also gave them up to uncleanness, in the lusts of their hearts, to dishonor their bodies among themselves, 25 who exchanged the truth of God for the lie, and worshiped and served the creature rather than the Creator, who is blessed forever. Amen.

---

[43] Abomination - By permission. From Merriam-Webster's Collegiate® Dictionary, 11th Edition ©2015 by Merriam-Webster, Inc. (www.Merriam-Webster.com)

26 For this reason God gave them up to vile passions. <u>For even their women exchanged the natural use for what is against nature.</u> 27 <u>Likewise also the men, leaving the natural use of the woman, burned in their lust for one another, men with men committing what is shameful, and receiving in themselves the penalty of their error which was due.</u> 28 And even as they did not like to retain God in their knowledge, <u>God gave them over to a debased mind, to do those things which are not fitting;</u>

29 being filled with all unrighteousness, sexual immorality, wickedness, covetousness, maliciousness; full of envy, murder, strife, deceit, evil-mindedness; they are whisperers, 30 backbiters, haters of God, violent, proud, boasters, inventors of evil things, disobedient to parents, 31 undiscerning, untrustworthy, unloving, unforgiving, unmerciful;

32 who, knowing the righteous judgment of God, that those who practice such things are deserving of death, not only do the same but also approve of those who practice them. - (Romans 1:24-32 NKJV)

There are two different government systems. God's Kingdom vs. Satan's Kingdom. Water and oil do not mix. What agreement is there between the righteous and unrighteous?

Do not be unequally yoked together with unbelievers. For what fellowship has righteousness with lawlessness? And what communion has light with darkness? - (2 Corinthians 6:14 NKJV)

You are all sons of light and sons of the day. We are neither of the night nor of darkness. - (1 Thessalonians 5:5 NKJV)

9 Do you not know that the unrighteous will not inherit the kingdom of God? Do not be deceived. Neither fornicators, nor idolaters, nor adulterers, nor homosexuals, nor sodomites, 10 nor thieves, nor covetous, nor drunkards, nor revilers, nor extortioners will inherit the kingdom of God. 11 And such were some of you. But you were washed, but you were sanctified, but you were justified in the name of the Lord Jesus and by the Spirit of our God. - (1 Corinthians 6:9-11 NKJV)

Merriam-Webster Changes Definition

Interesting to note, Merriam-Webster has added to the traditional definition of marriage. It now includes the following definition:

Marriage[44]:

... "a similar relationship between people of the same sex"...

..."the state of being united to a person of the same sex in a relationship like that of a traditional marriage"...

Look up in Merriam-Webster the definitions for the words "similar" and "like." Something "similar" will NEVER be "exactly" the same. The major reason heterosexual marriages are vastly different from homosexual acts, is due to the physiology and inability to produce offspring. People choosing to engage in homosexual acts do not have the ability to procreate. When a man and a man or a woman and a woman participate solely in homosexual acts, procreation is an impossibility.

The only way procreation would be possible under such a scenario, is if in the depravity and wickedness of man, "modern science" circumvents God's original design. There will never be a baby produced from two homosexuals' DNA. Artificial insemination could take place from a male to a female, but that is still not qualified as homosexual procreation.

What if science tampers with humanity? Is mankind actually attempting to go in a direction allowing a man to become pregnant and a woman altered to produce sperm?

Even then, the homosexual relationship would not be justified as marriage in the eyes of the Creator of Heaven and Earth. It would only serve to reveal man's wicked attempt to justify its actions apart from God's original design.

---

[44] Marriage - By permission. From Merriam-Webster's Collegiate® Dictionary, 11th Edition ©2015 by Merriam-Webster, Inc. (www.Merriam-Webster.com)

God created man and woman to come together as one flesh. Men and women have distinct traits and qualities. When a man and woman come together, the two become one, where man is weak, the woman is strong and where the woman is weak, the man is strong. Even though dictionary companies are doing their best to associate marriage with people engaging in homosexual acts, the truth is, homosexuals will never fit under the definition of marriage. It would be better for them to create a new term, than poorly attempt to identify their relationship under the umbrella of "marriage." Same-sex relationships will always invariably be different from heterosexual marriage relationships. The only similarity is the reality that there are two humans attempting to define a relationship and having it recognized by law. Outside of that, nothing is similar.

Hate Speech

There may be unbelievers (perhaps some professing believers) reading the preceding words and thinking to themselves, "This is hate speech! This guy is ... fill in the blank." I am sorry you might be believing those thoughts and feelings right now. Be assured, nothing could be further from the truth. Again, the purpose of this book is to ask the tough questions and uncover the truth, communicating that truth from a place of love. In fact, speaking the truth is love. If you happen to be struggling at the moment, please pause. Take a deep breath, take a step back from the emotions and keep reading.

Perhaps an in-depth explanation will help bring forth greater understanding of these thoughts and ideas. The world has become increasingly concerned regarding the vocabulary used from one human towards another human. The term "politically correct" is basically another name for "word police." It is interesting to point out how the United States of America was actually founded upon the very ability to express "freedom of speech." Some individuals in this country desire to remove this major founding principle necessary for a "free people" to exist. The so called "tolerant" preachers have become seemingly the most "intolerant" of words that were written over 2000 years ago. Words in which societies have been formed by and flourished under. Those preaching "tolerance," demonstrate their "intolerance," when it comes to views opposing sinful lifestyles as written in the Bible. Sadly, people want their sin... to their own detriment.

Personally, I hate sin, all sin. Everything God calls sin, I hate, because He hates it and He alone is good. Sin is a <u>particular action or spoken word</u> that goes against what God calls good, righteous and just. It is important to point out people are separate from their actions. People are not sin. However, humans do sinful things. Everyone has sinned and fallen short of the glory of God.

Sin[45] *a* : an offense against religious or moral law

b : an action that is or is felt to be highly reprehensible <it's a *sin* to waste food>

c : an often serious shortcoming : fault

2 *a* : *transgression of the law of God*   *b* : a vitiated state of human nature in which the self is estranged from God

You might ask, "Why do you hate sin? What is so bad about sin?" Sin causes separation from God, which can lead to death.

The Bible says, "The wages of sin is death." I do not know about you, but personally I do not appreciate death, specifically the death of people around me. Depending on the relationship, death can be quite heartbreaking. I have lost friends and family <u>to death and have cried du</u>e to the sadness of loss. Physical

[45] Sin - By permission. From Merriam-Webster's Collegiate® Dictionary, 11th Edition ©2015 by Merriam-Webster, Inc. (www.Merriam-Webster.com)

death is only one example of the many different kinds of death that exist. Physical, emotional and spiritual are all examples of different kinds of death.

Mankind was created specifically for male and female relationships to allow the continuation of humanity from generation to generation. If the population became strictly homosexual, the entire human race would become extinct within 100 years, because no reproduction would take place.

Practicing homosexuality is a choice, just like heterosexuals who choose to have sex outside the confines of a marriage relationship, commonly identified as fornication. In fact, John Hopkins University announced in 2016 after doing a study, that there is no such thing as homosexual genes or being born "gay." As much as media might suggest people are born homosexual, it simply is not true. Generally speaking, people practicing homosexuality were either abused sexually as children or later chose to participate in this sin willingly. Both homosexuality and fornication are forms of sexual immorality. These actions, continually practiced, can lead to death.

Again, this is not hate speech towards people or even from God towards mankind. Rather, this is actually defining love by providing knowledge of right vs. wrong. Believe it or not, God loves mankind. He loves you. He loves me. He loves all of mankind. How do I know God loves people?

"For God so loved the world that He gave His only begotten Son, that whoever believes in Him should not perish but have everlasting life." (John 3:16 NKJV)

God provided the Bible to mankind so they would understand good actions from evil actions. The Bible can be looked at as an instruction manual for life. God's great love for humanity is laid out in this book. In reading the Bible, we discover a love story between the Creator and the created. He loves us so much He gave His Son so that we could be reconciled and restored to relationship with Him. You can talk to Him right now! He is that big. He sees and hears everything you say, do, and think. Be honest with Him. He can handle your honesty. In fact, He values and appreciates honesty.

Jesus laid down His life for sinners while they were still His enemy. I do not know what your current thoughts are regarding Jesus Christ. It is not too late to acknowledge Him as Lord (if you have not already) and make Him Master of your life. He is all-together good. His thoughts for you are as many as the grains of sand on the seashore, filled with grace, mercy and compassion.

Jesus says, *28"Come to Me, all you who labor and are heavy laden, and I will give you rest. 29 "Take My yoke upon you and learn from Me, for I am gentle and lowly in heart, and you will find rest for your souls. 30 "For My yoke is easy and My burden is light." (Matthew 11:28-30 NKJV)*

Born Again

Once born again, the believer is instantly translated from being a part of Satan's Kingdom into God's Kingdom. There is a new government to live for now. It is the Lordship of Jesus Christ, His Kingdom, Dominion and Government we are translated into.

3 Jesus answered and said to him, "Most assuredly, I say to you, unless one is born again, he cannot see the kingdom of God." 4 Nicodemus said to Him, "How can a man be born when he is old? Can he enter a second time into his mother's womb and be born?" 5 Jesus answered, "Most assuredly, I say to you, unless one is born of water and the Spirit, he cannot enter the kingdom of God. (John 3:3-5 NKJV)

9 that if you confess with your mouth the Lord Jesus and believe in your heart that God has raised Him from the dead, you will be saved. 10 For with the heart one believes unto righteousness, and with the mouth confession is made unto salvation. 11 For the Scripture says, "Whoever believes on Him will not be put to shame." ... 13 For "whoever calls on the name of the LORD shall be saved." (Romans 10:9-11, 13 NKJV)

Recognizing Same Sex Marriage

Initially, when I started to write this book, only five states (as well as The District of Columbia) allowed same sex couples to have a recognized union. Those states were: Massachusetts, Connecticut, Iowa, Vermont and New Hampshire. As of April 2015, there were a total of 37 states that recognized homosexual union. Just two months later on June 26th 2015, the U.S. Supreme Court ruling allowed homosexual union for all 50 states. Who knows what is next? On the basis of "equality" every other type of relationship must be condoned if homosexuals are granted permission to "marry," otherwise it could be considered discrimination. Incest, pedophilia and beastiality may eventually become common place because of the U.S. Supreme Court ruling.

The sin of homosexuality is one of the most dangerous and harmful sins to participate in because it leads to the destruction of humanity itself. Sexual immorality was punishable by death in the Old Testament (adultery, homosexuality, bestiality, etc.) because it was so harmful not only to the individual (STD's) but detrimental to the future well-being of society as a whole and jeopardizing everyone's way of life. God loves humanity so much He will even step in to protect us from ourselves by flooding the earth or destroying a city, such as Sodom and Gomorrah.

In closing, please know God loves everyone. All sins are forgivable, aside from the blasphemy of the Holy Spirit. Everyone has an opportunity to change their mind, to turn towards Jesus and His righteousness. Let us give the Word of God its rightful place in our hearts, families and homes today.

Joshua Paul

20

CHANGING YOUR NAME IS EASY

One of the biggest concerns in regards to not acquiring a marriage license is the ability to change one's name. Married couples want to function under their new relational status. Not having a marriage license does not keep a married couple from receiving that relational benefit. In the process of calling different state employees and asking many questions, it was made clear that there were other options available for changing one's name.

Trish's Testimony

This testimony is about a woman named Trish and her husband got married without a license. They chose not to sign the marriage license and actually did not tell their children until they were grown adults. In fact, Trish had explained that up until this point, she had only shared this information with a handful of people. Meeting Trish was a Divine appointment. Hearing her story and testimony was a tremendous answer to prayer. Thank You Jesus. I hope her story will offer clarity and direction for those wishing to change their name.

Leading into marriage, Trish's husband advocated for not signing the marriage license. All of the, "no marriage license talk," was new to her so she began to do a thorough investigation of the scriptures. She did not find one example in the Bible indicating that she needed a marriage license. Upon further prayer and study, she also came to the realization that there was nothing indicating this was a violation of God's will or His Word. Trish chose to trust her husband, as well as God, with the legalities of marriage without a license.

In my conversation with Trish, I had other questions: "Trish, how did you change your name? What about the paperwork with all the different legalities, etc.?" She said, "It was not a problem. Nobody ever asked me to prove my marriage. I simply assumed my husband's last name. When I went to the Social Security Administration to change the name on my social security card, I simply stated on the application that I had gotten married and filled out the "name change."

Once receiving the updated social security card, changing all the other documents was straight forward and without question. She changed her name on her driver's license and bank accounts. Both her and her husband received health insurance as a married couple. She admitted that she had been nervous throughout this process, however, there were no problems.

Apparently, people do not have to go to a judge to petition the court for a name change. Wow! The marriage license is not that big of a deal. People can marry and enjoy life, apart from the influence and involvement of the state. There are so many myths surrounding the state marriage license, it is mind-boggling.

Trish's story does not end there. Unfortunately, her husband filed for divorce sometime in the late 90's. To complete the divorce, they went before the state and filed within the family court system. <u>The court viewed their relationship, as a marriage, without question.</u> They divorced, though Trish did not desire this outcome. Nearly 20 years after the fact, she is still contending for restoration and reconciliation of her marriage and family. She believes that the only option is either to remain single or reconcile with her husband. Remarriage is not an option for her, because she believes that she is still in a covenant relationship to the man she married. This is based upon Jesus' words in Matthew 5.

This committed woman of God, did not need a marriage license to validate her covenant marriage relationship.

Though Trish's husband may not currently desire reconciliation, I am believing for the Living God to restore this marriage and family. Please send up a prayer for Trish and her husband right now. In fact, please pray for all marriages that are in need of reconciliation.

Prayer

Father in Heaven, I lift up Trish and her husband. I ask that you would restore and reconcile them to each other. I ask that you do a work in both Trish and her husband's life. Let every influencing spirit that is not of You, YHWH, be cast down right now and bound in the Lake of Fire. Thank You for letting Your Holy Spirit come into their lives in those empty places. Fill these vessels and temples for Your glory Jesus. LORD, please bring restoration to marriages and families across the face of the earth right now. In Jesus' name I pray. Amen.

Changing Your Name - Option #1

For women who want to assume their husband's name after the wedding, simply contact the Social Security Administration, fill out a name change application and wait for a new card. You can then use the new card to change your other documents.

Changing Your Name - Option #2

Request a court ordered legal name change.

I spoke with a friend of mine from Arizona named Lauren. She married her husband without applying for a marriage license. Lauren appealed the court for a name change, stating that she wanted the last name of her "spiritual life partner." This was the reason she gave for desiring a name change. The court approved her name change request. Both Trish and Lauren changed their names in different ways, but the outcome was the same – legal, successful and without a marriage license.

Lawful Name Change

These are the sequence of steps if you go through the court system.

1. Acquire Legal Name Change - Superior Court System

You will need to go to the court and apply for a legal name change. This process is fairly simple. There will be an application and a fee. A website to determine your state's name change process is: www.uslegalforms.com/changeofname The process and fee associated with each state is always a little different, so do your homework and follow the rules accordingly.

As an example, in the state of Kansas some of the restrictions listed from the website above are as follows:

"You may *not* obtain a name change in the state of Kansas for the purposes of avoiding debts, avoiding legal process, or to mislead or defraud any person. The district county court judge also reserves the right to deny your petition for name change, after reviewing the testimony, examining the evidence and reviewing the record."

2. Social Security Number

Most Americans today have a social security number. Once approved for a legal name change, then visit the Social Security Administration or their website. In the footer, is the link to the Social Security website for the form needed to change your name[46]. As you will read on the application for SS-5, simply put your new name in, put your previous name, your number and then fill out the rest. Mail the application in and wait to hear from them regarding your updated social security card.

3. Government ID

You will need to change your name on all of your government records. The driver's license, if you have one, or your state identification would be examples of what I am talking about

---

[46] http://www.socialsecurity.gov/forms/ss-5.pdf

here. Your passport is also another document you will want to update.

4. Financial Accounts

Once you have updated your social security card, government records, state driver's license, passport, etc., then it should be straight forward changing all other documents. Your banking, stock and insurance accounts will be the next most important things to change.

5. Bills and Employment

Updating your bills and other company accounts is the next move in this process of changing your name. Here is a sample list of places you may also want to update:

- Business
- Employer
- Electric and Utility Companies
- Any Legal Documents
- Credit Card Companies
- Post Office
- Landlord or Mortgage Companies
- Insurance Companies (auto, home, life)
- Doctor's Office
- Voter Registration
- Gym and Social Club Memberships
- Schools and Alumni Associations
- Email
- Social Websites, Facebook, Linkedin, Twitter, etc.

Concluding Comments

This book has attempted to answer the question, "What do we give to Caesar and what do give to God?" It seems clear, marriage is something that God created, not the government. Do we desire for our marriages to be fully set apart unto God, without any unnecessary governmental involvement? The marriage license is something we can easily do without. Our personal marriage relationship and covenant between our spouse and God alone, is fundamentally available in our society today. Will we as a people choose to be set apart?

Here are some additional reasons as to why signing the marriage license is less than an ideal covenant:

1. Calling what God created a criminal activity – the marriage of a man and woman.

2. Yoking yourself to a three-party relationship with the state and their spouse. (Some make the argument that this is a polygamous relationship.)

3. The couple is knowingly or unknowingly admitting they are not competent to handle their own affairs.

4. Legally makes the state the parent over the marriage and the children to follow.

5. There is no additional security in having a marriage license vs. common law marriage, from a legal standpoint. If anything, there is less security, because of the "no-fault" divorce legislation mentioned earlier.

For those looking for other options found in common law marriage, people can be assured:

1. Marriage between a man and woman has always been legal in the eyes of God and mankind.
2. Common law marriage is legal in all 50 states.
3. Common law keeps an unholy government out of the intimate details of your marriage relationship.
4. Couples are able to receive the same "benefits" as those with marriage licenses – such as filing taxes, buying homes or acquiring health insurance.

Followers of Jesus are being confronted with the questions:

- How important is marriage?
- Is marriage worth fighting for as God designed it?
- Will believers keep marriages together for the sake of their spouses, families and society?
- Will God's people keep their commitments, as unto the LORD?

The body of Christ is the moral standard for society. Marriage is not just for an individual, not just for a couple, not just for a family, but for the LORD and all of society. There is strength added to society when a man and woman stay together in a committed relationship. Will the people of God raise the standard of marriage to what it was always intended to demonstrate? Marriage is the most significant relationship anyone could enter into, reflecting the very image and nature of God. The marriage covenant was always designed to represent a picture of oneness in God. The Bible communicates clearly, this relationship is not easy and there will be challenges. For those of you who say, "Yes!" to this relationship, can you think of a better cause to fight for?

This book is intended to provide a point of reflection as to the foundational truths surrounding marriage according to the Word of God. Individuals and couples still need to seek first the Kingdom of God and His righteousness throughout their marriage. Husband and wife each have a responsibility towards the other within their relationship. Blaming the success or failure of a relationship on a marriage license or a lack thereof is not the point of this writing. The point is to simply pursue God's highest and best perspective entering into marriage, with a solid foundation for a new life together.

Concluding Prayer

Father in Heaven, please strengthen Your people. Let us be a people of perseverance, commitment, integrity and character. Let us be a people committed to You and Your Word. Let us seek first the kingdom of God and Your righteousness. Expose all deception taking place within our lives. Let us be a people that take responsibility for our decisions. Holy Spirit, help us. Holy Spirit help marriages. Help marriages become what they can only be with Your presence. Let us be a people of purity. Purify Your Bride, LORD Jesus. The Spirit and the Bride say, "Come LORD Jesus come!" I ask in Your name, Jesus. Amen.

Sample Marriage Certificates & Covenants

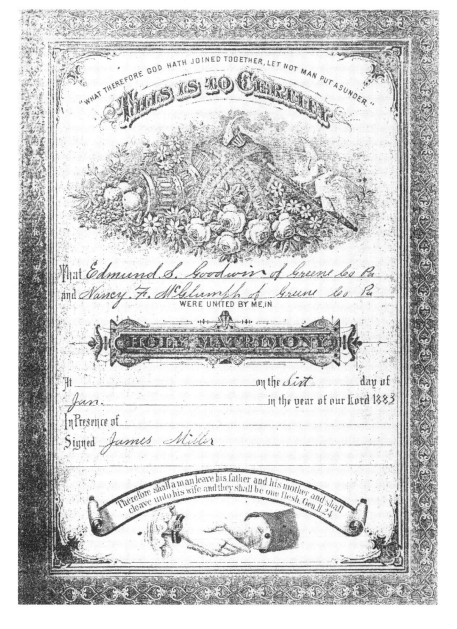

Marriage Covenant

Holy Matrimony is to be honored by all, being a covenant and the creation of a sovereign family, annuls heretofore-covenanted family authority. Both male and female are to leave their father and mother's home, blessed by them and united one to another becoming one flesh, thus consummating said covenant. Believing that YHWH (God) established marriage as a covenant relationship, a sacred lifelong promise, reflecting our unconditional love for one another and believing that He intends for marriage to reflect His promise to never leave us or forsake us.

This marriage covenant is created in the sight of the Most High God, the Church and family. This is to be witnessed unto the commitment of love, being ordained by the Sovereign Lord Most High, binding between _____ and_____ together in holy matrimony before God and man on this day _____ and year _____ in _____.

"What God has joined together let no man separate." Mark 10:9 Therefore, all who seek to make war against said covenant shall battle with YHWH, who doth uphold this bond by His eternal power and deity. To YHWH alone be the glory.

We recognize and acknowledge this is a life long covenant and commitment as communicated in the Bible, by Yeshua our Messiah and Savior.

Husband_____   Wife_____

Witness_____   Witness_____

Witness_____

Keep in mind, you are free to customize and add scripture, promises, etc. This is nothing more than a sample. It's good to have 3 witnesses sign it, date, location, and husband and wife sign the document as well.

Marriage Covenant

The family, being established by covenant and blessed of God before, but apprehending in seed form, both Church and magistrate, is to be acknowledged as the foundation of all society by God's most perfect order and ordination. From the beginning, the family has been the means by which our great God has seen fit to extend His dominion, His presence and fellowship, unto the ends of the earth. This covenant is drawn in the sight of the Almighty God, the Church and our parents, to be a witness unto the commitment and love, being ordained by the Almighty God, which bind Groom and Bride together in holy matrimony.

Gen 2 : 8-24
Gen 1 : 26-30
Gen 17: 9-10
Isaiah 44: 3

Acts 2: 39 1
Cor 7:14
Malachi: 2:14

Holy matrimony, to be honored by all, being a covenant and the creation of a new sovereign family, annuls heretofore covenanted family authority. Both man and wife are to leave father and mother, being blessed by both, and be united one unto another becoming one flesh, thus consummating said covenant.

Heb 13: 4
Gen 2: 24
Matt 19: 4 -6

Mark 10: 6-9
Eph 5: 13

The husband being called and commanded of our Lord, is to love his wife as Christ Jesus Himself does love His body, the Church, thus committing his life unto her, The wife being heir of the grace of life, and in order to hinder not his prayers, the husband is to honor her as unto the weaker vessel, leading not with a strong hand, but as a servant, without wrath and disputation, seeking always the imitation of our Lord, Who is head over every man.

Eph 5: 25-33
1 Peter 3: 7
Luke 22: 26
1 Timothy 2: 8

Phil 2: 11
1 Cor 11: 9
Col 1: 15-20

The wife, being called and commanded of our Lord, is to love her husband, being in submission to his godly headship. She is to respect him, acknowledge and uphold his authority in the family, helping him toward fulfilling both the cultural mandate and the commission delivered unto the saints by our Lord.

Eph 5: 22-24
Eph 5: 33
1 Cor 11: 3

Gen 2: 18
Matt 28: 18-20

Being captivated by each other's love, content and satisfied, both husband and wife are to recognize and forever abide in their mutual dependence in the Lord, not depriving one another of any marital gift, for love never fails. Out of love, both are to believe and obey the commands of our Lord, said commands being not burdensome, through the power of the Holy Spirit.

Prov 5: 15-19
Song of Songs
1 Cor 11: 11
1 Cor 12: 1

1 Cor 7: 3-5
1 Cor 13:4-8
2 John 6
Romans 8: 3-4

Being that God has seen fit to transmit His provision and covenant by means of the family, both husband and wife are under obligation to instruct in all diligence the Word of God unto the children granted them of the Lord. This Word, being revealed as the Holy Scriptures, brings life and potence, wisdom unto salvation, transforming those who abide in it, equipping them unto every good work.

Deut 6: 6-7
Acts 2: 39
Psalms 127, 128
Heb 4: 12

2 Tim 3:14-15
Psalm 1: 1-3
2 Tim 3:16-17

That this covenant is instituted by God is to be acknowledged by all—"What God has joined together, let not man separate" Mark 10:9—therefore, all who seek to make war against said covenant shall battle with the Almighty, Who doth uphold this bond by His Eternal Power and Deity.

Matt 19: 3-9
1 Cor 7:10-11

Col 1:15-20
Psalm 2

To God alone be the glory!

In the presence of the Triune God and these witnesses, with great joy and solemnity we mutually bind ourselves this day, in a holy covenant of marriage. With a constant reliance on God's grace and resting in His love we promise to love and serve one another consistent with the above principles communicated to us by Almighty God, himself. This we shall do as long as we both shall live. We solemnly swear this vow in the name of the Father, and of the Son and of the Holy Ghost and seal the same by our hands this thirteenth day of November in the year of our Lord Two-Thousand and sixteen at Spitfire Acres in the city of Southhaven, county of DeSoto , state of Mississippi.

The Groom _____ The Bride _____

Witness _____ Witness _____

Witness _____ Witness _____

Provided by, Covenant Community Church a redemptive society in

Whitehall, Montana: www.truthinliving.org

English Translation Of An Orthodox Ketubah Marriage Contract

On the _____ day of the week, the _____ day of the month _____ in the year five thousand seven hundred and _____ since the creation of the world, the era according to which we reckon here in the city of _____ that _____ son of _____ said to this (virgin) _____ daughter of _____: "Be my wife according to the practice of Moses and Israel, and I will cherish, honor, support and maintain you in accordance with the custom of Jewish husbands who cherish, honor, support and maintain their wives faithfully. And I here present you with the marriage gift of (for virgins), (two hundred) silver zuzim, which belongs to you, according to the law of Moses and Israel; and I will also give you your food, clothing and necessities, and live with you as husband and wife according to universal custom." And Miss _____, this (virgin), consented and became his wife. The trousseau that she brought to him from her (father's) house in silver, gold, valuables, clothing, furniture and bedclothes, all this _____, the said bride-groom accepted in the sum of (one hundred) silver pieces, and _____, the bridegroom, consented to increase this amount from his own property with the sum of (one hundred) silver pieces, making in all (two hundred) silver pieces. And thus said _____, the bridegroom: "The responsibility of this marriage contract, of this trousseau, and of this additional sum, I take upon myself and my heirs after me, so that they shall be paid from the best part of my property and possession that I have beneath the whole heaven, that which I now possess or may here after acquire. All my property, real and personal, even the shirt from my back, shall be mortgaged to secure the payment of this marriage contract, of the trousseau, and of the addition made to it, during my lifetime and after my death, from the present day and forever." _____, the bridegroom, has taken upon himself the responsibility of this marriage contract.

Attested to_____

Witness Attested to_____ Witness

Permission of use Granted by CJFM.org
MESSIANIC PERSPECTIVES- JULY AUGUST 2011

Without going into too much detail, please know and realize the price and value of silver is very much manipulated, trading far below what supply and demand might otherwise indicate is true fair market value. Some people claim the fair market value of silver should be anywhere from $500-$2,000 per ounce. If this is the case that would bring the Bride price to $10,000-$40,000, rather than the current market value of $350-1,000.

Addendum - Alabama Abolishes Marriage License

In February 2016, Alabama introduced Senate Bill (SB143.) This bill passed April 21, 2016 with a 23-3 vote. The legislation abolishes all requirements to obtain a marriage license in the state of Alabama. Probate judges would simply record marriages between two individuals with a signed affidavit.

This decision has a two-fold affect. It would render void the edicts of the federal supreme court judges over this issue of marriage. Alabama's ruling would also limit the state's role in defining, regulating and identifiying marriage relationships. Governmental employees will not be forced to do something that goes against their conscience or religious beliefs.

Alabama essentially recognizes that it should have a minimal role in the legalities of marriage. Alabama's leadership has a terrific grasp of law and its role in the legal status of relationship. If all the states took this approach, the American people would be well-served surrounding the topic of legal marriage.

Hopefully more states will follow Alabama's lead. Although this may not happen, due to politicians looking out for the interest of the state, before the interest of the people. Letting go of millions of dollars in revenue each year is not easy for most government bodies.

More information on this ruling can be optained from the article noted below:

http://blog.tenthamendmentcenter.com/2016/04/alabama-house-committee-passes-bill-eliminating-government-marriage-licensing/

Recommended Reading and Resources

The Holy Bible, NKJV, Thomas Nelson Publishing

Longing For Eden, Mike and Anne Rizzo - marriagelongingforeden.com

The 5 Love Languages, Gary D. Chapman

Supernatural Marriage, Dan Wilson - supernaturalmarriage.org

Sacred Marriage, Gary Thomas

Love and Respect, Dr. Emmerson Eggerichs

Boundaries, Dr. Henry Cloud & Dr. John Townsend

Man of Steel and Velvet, Dr. Aubrey Andelin

Biblical Foundations of Freedom, Art Mathias

Freedom Immersion and Marriage Immersion, by Freedom City Church in Tacoma Washington - citycentral.org

Nothing Hidden Ministries, P.O.Box 992383, Redding, CA 96099 nothinghidden.com

The Cleansing Seminar, Dr. Timothy Davis - Cleansing the Church Ministries: PO Box 8326, Mission Hills, CA 91346 USA 818.833.7999

His Holy Church.org
http://www.hisholychurch.org/declarations/marriage/index.php/

Reference

Chapter 1 - The Question

See Matthew 22:17-21 NKJV
See Matthew 22:21 NIV
See Matthew 22:21 The Interlinear Bible - Greek/English
See Matthew 19:6 NKJV

Chapter 2 - The Journey Continues

See Joshua 9:3-5, 7-15, 18-19, 23 NKJV
See Exodus 23:24, 32-33 NIV
See Matthew 5:11, 44; 10:34-38; NKJV
See John 15:20 NKJV

Chapter 3 - Where Did Marriage Originate

Genesis 2:18; 21-25 NKJV

Chapter 4 - The Purpose of Marriage

See Genesis 2:18; 21-25; *38:9-10* NKJV
See Genesis 9:1, 7 NKJV
See Psalm 127:3 NKJV
See 2 Chronicles 7:13-15 NKJV
See Malachi 2:10-16 NKJV

See 1 Corinthians 7:5 NKJV
See 1Timothy 2:15 NKJV
http://en.wikipedia.org/wiki/Total_fertility_rate
www.thebirthcontrolmovie.com
http://www.tlc.com/tv-shows/19-kids-and-counting

Chapter 5 – Families & Preparation for Marriage

See Ephesians 5:25-29 NKJV
See 1 Peter 3:3-4
See Titus 2:1-5; 6-8 NKJV

Chapter 6 - Hebrew Courtship and Wedding Formalities

See *Song 8:7 NKJV*
See Exodus 20:12 NKJV
See Ephesians 5:25, 6:2 NKJV

Messianic Perspectives July-August 2011 A publication of CJF
Ministrieshttps://www.scribd.com/fullscreen/66981748?access_key=key-
6qcykw38wo4pc7hhd0q&allow_share=true&escape=false&show_recommendatio
ns=false&view_mode=scroll

http://www.bible.ca/marriage/ancient-jewish-three-stage-weddings-and-marriage-
customs-ceremony-in-the-bible.htm

http://www.chabad.org/library/article_cdo/aid/477321/jewish/Kiddushin-
Betrothal.htm

Chapter 7 – Ceremony

See Genesis 2:12-15; 21-25; 24:41, 51, 53-54, 57-61, 63-67; 29:15, 18-23, 25-28, 30
NKJV

Chapter 8 - Conception

Conception of a Child, All Heaven Celebrates the Moment; T. Leverett - March 22,
2010

96 U.S. 76 - 24 L.Ed. 826 MEISTER v. MOORE October Term, 1877

Chapter 9 - Origin and History of Marriage License

See Matthew 23:9

See John 3:3, 3:16

See Acts 8:37

The Marriage License by Dr. Benjamin E. TownsendAmerican Uniform Marriage and Marriage License Act

https://carm.org/list-of-roman-catholic-false-teachings
http://www.usccb.org/beliefs-and-teachings/what-we-believe/catechism/catechism-of-the-catholic-church/epub/index.cfm
http://www.vatican.va/archive/ENG0015/_INDEX.HTM
http://www.chick.com/information/religions/catholicism/
http://en.wikipedia.org/wiki/Marriage_license

"The Uniform Marriage and Divorce Act" (UMDA)

http://www.uniformlaws.org/shared/docs/Marriage%20and%20Divorce%20Act/UMDA%201973.pdf

Chapter 10 - Parens Patriae

Black's Law - Parens Patriae

Reference: TheFreeDictionary © 2015 by Farlex, Inc.

http://legal-dictionary.thefreedictionary.com/Parens+Patriae

http://www.breakingchristiannews.com/articles/display_art.html?ID=15067

http://medicalkidnap.com/2014/12/03/local-king-5-news-reports-on-rengo-family-children-being-medically-kidnapped/

http://www.hisholychurch.org/declarations/marriage/index.php/

Chapter 11 - Is the Government Holy?

See Exodus 19:6 NKJVSee 1 Peter 1:15-16 NKJV

See 1 Peter 2:9 NKJV

See Ephesians 6:12 NKJV

See John 17:11-19 NKJV

See Psalm 37See Psalm 139

See Jeremiah 29:11
See Deuteronomy 7:1-16
See Proverbs 25:2

Chapter 12 - Permission from the State

See 1 Timothy 4:1,3 NKJV

See Proverbs 3:5-7; 3:8-10NKJV

See John 10:10 NKJV

See 1Peter 5:8 NKJV

See Hosea 4:1-10 NKJV

See Habakkuk 2:2 NKJV

http://quotes.liberty-tree.ca/quote_blog/Peter.Hoagland.Quote.0FD8

http://www.wnd.com/2011/11/372409/#WovBFEAVQKBpU8SJ.99

https://www.ohiobar.org/ForPublic/Resources/LawFactsPamphlets/Pages/LawFactsPamphlet-35.aspx

96 U.S. 76 - 24 L.Ed. 826 MEISTER v. MOORE October Term, 1877

http://caselaw.findlaw.com/al-court-of-civil-appeals/1325717.html

Linneman v. Linneman, 1 Ill.App.2d 48, 50, 116 N.E.2d 182, 183 (1953),

Van Koten v. Van Koten, 323 Ill. 323, 326, 154 N.E. 146 (1926). ☐

Linneman, 1 Ill.App.2d at 50, 116 N.E.2d at 183. ☐

http://caselaw.findlaw.com/il-court-of-appeals/1486817.html#sthash.4KofxrrT.dpuf

https://amiracle42sisters.wordpress.com/2015/01/21/please-join-the-truth-train/

Chapter 13 - Adhesion Contract

Black's Law Dictionary, 10th ed. 2014

http://digitalcommons.law.ggu.edu/cgi/viewcontent.cgi?article=1877&context=ggulrev

Chapter 14 - The Fraud Matter

See Matthew 19:8 NKJV

96 U.S. 76 - 24 L.Ed. 826 MEISTER v. MOORE October Term, 1877
https://supreme.justia.com/cases/federal/us/96/76/case.html
http://thelawdictionary.org/directory/

http://www.nationmaster.com/graph/peo_div_rat-people-divorce-rate

https://en.wikipedia.org/wiki/Religion_in_the_United_states

http://www.cookcountyclerk.com/vitalrecords/marriagelicenses/Pages/default.aspx

http://www.merriamwebster.com/dictionary/must

http://www.1215.org/lawnotes/misc/marriage/meister_v_moore_96_us_76.pdf

http://www.merriam-webster.com/dictionary/fraud

Chapter 15 - Laws of the Land

http://www.billofrightsinstitute.org/founding-documents/bill-of-rights/

See Romans 13:1-4

(MEYER v. STATE OF NEBRASKA, 262 U.S. 390 (1923)

https://supreme.justia.com/cases/federal/us/262/390/case.html

See 1 Peter 5:8 NKJV

Uniform Marriage and Marriage License Act

Declaration of Independence – In Congress, July 4, 1776

http://www.archives.gov/exhibits/charters/declaration_transcript.html

Chapter 16 - Types of Legal Marriage

Common Law Marriage And It's Development in the United states - by Otto Erwin Koegel

http://www.originalintent.org/edu/marriage.php

Supreme Court case of Meister Vs. Moore in 1877Black's Law Dictionary, 10th ed. 2014

http://www.1215.org/lawnotes/misc/marriage/index.html

http://www.1215.org/lawnotes/misc/marriage/marriage-certificate.pdf

http://www.1215.org/lawnotes/misc/marriage/original_intent-common_law_marriage.pdf

Chapter 17 - How Can I Get Out?

American Uniform Marriage and Marriage License Act

See Romans 8:1 NKJVSee Acts 16:20-24 NKJVSee Ezekiel 22:23-26 NKJVSee James 4:4-10 NKJV

Chapter 18- Vows, Adultery & Divorce

See Psalm 15:1-5, 119 NKJV

See Matthew 5:29, 33-37 NIV

See Exodus 20:4-6,14 NKJV

See Leviticus 20:10 NKJV

See Deuteronomy 5:18 NKJV

See Proverbs 6:32 NKJV

See Jeremiah 3; 23:14-15 NKJV

See Ezekiel 23:37 NKJV

See Hosea 4NKJV

See Matthew 5:27-30; 10:28; *5:31-32; 19:3-10; 5:27-37* NKJV

See Revelation 2:20-23 NKJV

See Galatians 5:16

See James 4:4-6 NKJV

See John 8:3-11 NKJV

Meister vs. Moore in 1877

Chapter 19 - The Homosexual License

See Leviticus 20:13 NKJV

See Romans 1:24-32, *10:9-11, 13* NKJV

See 2 Corinthians 6:14 NKJV
See 1Thessalonians 5:5 NKJV

See 1Corinthians 6:9-11 NKJV

See John 3:16, *3:3-5* NKJV
See Matthew 11:28-30 NKJV

http://www.care2.com/causes/what-states-allow-gay-marriage.html

http://gaymarriage.procon.org/view.resource.php?resourceID=004857

http://www.cnn.com/2013/05/28/us/same-sex-marriage-fast-facts

Chapter 20 - Changing Your Name is Easy

www.iowacourts.gov

http://www.change.name

http://www.uslegalforms.com/changeofname/

http://www.socialsecurity.gov/ssnumber/ss5.htm - Call - 1-800-772-1213

http://www.azleg.gov/ArizonaRevisedStatutes.asp?Title=1

https://www.legis.iowa.gov/DOCS/Central/Guides/marriage.pdf

https://www.ksbar.org/?marriage_divorce

Disclaimer:

This information is provided and sold with the knowledge that the publisher and author do not offer any legal or other professional advice. In the case of a need for any such expertise consult with an appropriate legal professional. This book does not contain all information available on the written subject matter. This book has not been created to be specific to any individual's or organizations' situation or needs. Every effort has been made to make this book as accurate as possible. However, there may be typographical, grammatical and or content errors. Therefore, this book should serve only as a general guide and not as the ultimate source of subject information. This book contains information that might be dated and is intended only to educate and entertain. The author and publisher shall have no liability or responsibility to any person or entity regarding any loss or damage incurred, or alleged to have incurred, directly or indirectly, by the information contained in this book. The author does not assume and hereby disclaims any liability to any party for any loss, damage, or disruption caused by errors or omissions, whether such errors or omissions result from accident, negligence, or any other cause. You hereby agree to be bound by this disclaimer or you may return this book in new condition. No part of this book may be reproduced or transmitted in any form or by any means, electronic or mechanical, including photocopying, recording or by any information storage and retrieval system, without written permission from the author.

ABOUT THE AUTHOR

Joshua Paul grew up in a Christian home, attended a non-denominational Christian church, read the Bible and prayed in Jesus' name. Graduating from a top 10 business school, he launched out into the world of business ownership by continuing with his online eCommerce business, which he started at the age of 20. Joshua also has years of experience working in the entertainment industry as a model and actor. Using God's gifts and talents, his goal was to reach those who would possibly never set foot in a church building. Eventually, Joshua began working with Christian non-profit ministries on a full-time basis where the Lord further developed, refined and cultivated his relationship with Jesus. Working between ministry and the marketplace, Joshua now desires to use his gifts and talents to develop as a philanthropist, entrepreneur and minister of the Word.

For readers who have appreciated and become informed by this book, look for Joshua Paul's previous book "Marriage License Fraud: What every Christian couple should know before signing a marriage license." "Marriage License Fraud" is a condensed version of this book highlighting the direct issues surrounding the marriage license.

Contact:
http://TheBiblicalMarriage.com
JesusisLord@TheBiblicalMarriage.com

Printed in Great Britain
by Amazon

44963286R00122